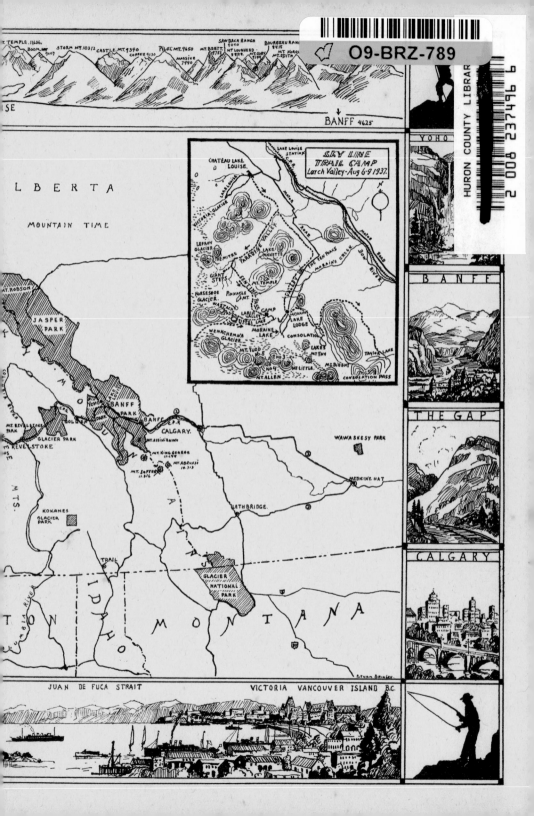

AWAY TO
THE CANADIAN ROCKIES
and BRITISH COLUMBIA

Cathedral Peak from Lake O'Hara

AWAY TO
THE CANADIAN ROCKIES
and BRITISH COLUMBIA

BY

GORDON BRINLEY

Author of

"AWAY TO THE GASPÉ"
"AWAY TO CAPE BRETON"
"AWAY TO QUEBEC"

ILLUSTRATED BY

D. PUTNAM BRINLEY

DODD, MEAD & COMPANY
NEW YORK   1938

PRINTED IN THE UNITED STATES OF AMERICA
BY THE VAIL-BALLOU PRESS, INC., BINGHAMTON, N. Y.

WARNING

TO:

ARCHAEOLOGISTS

BOTANISTS

ENGINEERS

ETHNOGRAPHERS

ETHNOLOGISTS

GEOGRAPHERS

GEOLOGISTS

HISTORIANS

METEOROLOGISTS

NATURALISTS

MOUNTAIN CLIMBERS, GRADES A, B, AND C

PASS AT YOUR OWN RISK

By order of
The Duchess and Dan

CONTENTS

CONTENTS

ILLUSTRATIONS

[ix]

ILLUSTRATIONS

AWAY TO
THE CANADIAN ROCKIES
and BRITISH COLUMBIA

CHAPTER I

BAREFACED SIREN

ONE June morning of 1937 I was painting at my easel in the New Canaan studio, sweet air drifting in through open doors and windows, when a sound of footsteps in the balcony made me turn, and I saw, coming down the stairway, a figure dressed in blue denim overalls, plaid shirt, and riding boots; a wide-brimmed Stetson hat was set at a rakish angle over a pair of hazel eyes. The Duchess, gone Wild West!

"How do you like me, Dan?" she asked, skipping gaily down the last steps of the stair into the big, cool room.

"What the heck, Duchess!" I exclaimed inelegantly, laying down my brushes, not too pleased to have been interrupted in one of my rare creative moments. "Have we been hooked for a costume party tonight?"

"No, Dan, you're safe," she answered, laughing, her head thrown back; "it's only that I've been up in the attic." Sticking her hands into the overall pockets she began to stride around as she talked. "You see, the mail came awhile ago and brought me a letter from a strange man."

"How strange?" I asked.

"Exactly what I wanted to find out," she replied, "so I went up to the attic—"

"Why is it," I interrupted, "that the slightest emergency, and especially the rising temperature of summer, invariably sends women up into their attics? On the Fourth of July, Duchess, I fully expect you will have gone clean through attic and roof, and that I shall find you seated on the ridge-pole of the house poring over a family album!" The picture conjured by these words was too much for the Duchess's sense of humour. Doubling up with laughter, she sank into the nearest chair; her hat fell off and rolled along the floor, and I caught it on the toe of my shoe, asking, as I lobbed it back to her, "But what is the meaning of this?"

"I'm coming to it," she replied. "You see, Dan, I was hunting for my book on handwriting analysis. I wanted to get the low-down on the autograph hunter."

"Then you're a long way off the point, Duchess," I exclaimed. "What in time have those riding boots"—pointing to the ones she was wearing—"got to do with graphology?"

"Why, the boots and the book were side by side in a trunk! Storage, Dan, like adversity, makes strange bedfellows. When I saw these nice old things"—sticking the said boots out in front of her—"I felt a positive itch to put them on; when the boots were on, I thought, what fun to get into the whole outfit—and here I am!"

"Yes," I replied, "here you are, looking like little An-
nie Oakley with no place to go."

"Mercy!" exclaimed the Duchess, jumping up, "I
have to catch a train to New York—I'm promised to the
Tyrells for luncheon." And grabbing her hat she made
a dash to the stairs. Half way to the balcony she glanced
down, and, noting my expression (I hate to eat alone),
stopped and, leaning over the stair rail, gave me a smile
as she said:

"Don't look so forlorn, darling. You shall have a nice
bone all to yourself out on the south terrace—I've told
Iles—and I promise not to be late in getting home."

With a glance at my watch I called, "Better hurry or
you'll miss your train, and if you're not back by six
o'clock I'll notify the police!"

The Duchess made an amusing face at me, then, mod-
ulating her voice in approved radio style, she sang, "Good
by-e-e-e," and the next instant disappeared from sight.

About five o'clock of that sunny afternoon I was sitting
in the shade of the big rock maple near the river, enjoying a cup of coffee that had been brought to me there,
when, looking toward the house, I saw the Duchess
standing on the south terrace. Waving a hand to me, she
ran down the stone steps into the garden and came
quickly along the green centre alley that was bordered

[3]

with bright flowers of early summer.

"Right in the nick of time, Duchess," I said, placing a chair for her.

"Thanks, Dan." She sat down and, taking off her hat, tossed it, together with a large Manilla envelope, onto the grass. "How lovely it is here!" she exclaimed. "Why does one streak back to cities when there are gardens and rivers to enjoy? Why should we ever leave a place like this?"

"I'm asking you," I replied, pouring out a cup of coffee and handing it across the metal table to the Duchess. She took the cup, saying, "The very thing I want," and then, with a gesture indicating the envelope:

"You haven't asked what is in my package. I'll give you two guesses—no, I'd better tell you the whole story."

"Yes, give me the story, Duchess," I said. "I've been guessing with paints and brushes ever since you left me this morning."

"Well, then—at the luncheon today, as we were enjoying a fish course, one of the ladies present told a tall story about catching trout in a certain lake way out West in the Canadian Rockies. As they talked I thought of you. What interested me, of course, were her references to the marvellous scenery which surrounded the fish; she really got me excited, and I made up my mind to find out for myself something about the Rocky Moun-

tain area in Canada. Later, on my way to the Grand
Central Station, I stopped in at the office of the Canadian Pacific Railway and found a man who didn't mind
answering questions. He loaded me up—or should one
say down?—with 'literature' on the subject of fishing,
hiking, and"—with a side glance at me—"trail riding."

"Ha, ha, Duchess!" I sang out. "The boots have it!
You've been trying to divert my attention by dragging
a nice little red herring—I mean a trout—across the
conversation; but the real subject of your investigation
was trail riding, not fishing. Come now, be honest, wasn't
it, Duchess?" She went off into a gale of laughter, asking:

"Is there any earthly reason why trail riding and fishing shouldn't go together? And by the way"—inno-
cently—"I brought you a present; it's waiting in the
studio to surprise you."

"That's certainly jolly of you, Duchess!" I exclaimed,
getting up. "I'm wondering what it can be."

"Not yet, Dan," she said, pulling me down again;
"wait till I've shown you what I have here." And picking up the envelope she opened it and pulled out a
handful of brightly coloured folders and pamphlets.

"I'm not psychic," I remarked, "but it seems to me
we have been in this situation before, only the setting
was different." But she wasn't listening to me. Tossing
on the table, one after another, brilliantly designed pieces

[5]

of publicity, the Duchess, excited now, asked:

"Look, Dan, how do these appeal to you—'Trout Fishing in Marvel Lake,' 'Fishing in Lake Wapta,' 'Fisherman's Paradise: Consolation Lake,' 'Salmon Fishing at Victoria Island, B.C.'?" They were as powerful in allure as seed catalogues.

"What's the black and white one?" I asked, reaching for a pamphlet with a stunning photograph on its cover, and read as I picked it up: "Bulletin 46. Trail Riders of the Canadian Rockies." Beneath the picture it said, "Those who are planning to join the Trail Ride to Mt. Assiniboine this summer," etc.

"You barefaced siren," I exclaimed, flipping over pages that showed a map of the proposed five-day ride and pictures that illustrated verses in which the whole story of a "ride" was cleverly told, also a photograph of a camp at Forty Mile Creek showing the Indian tepees in which the riders slept at night.

"Turn over the page," urged the Duchess. ("She must have studied this thing coming home in the train," I thought, as I did so.)

"There," she said, "look at that pretty girl shaking hands with two Indian chiefs in full regalia. I wonder if I would have the courage to do that? Did you ever see such beautiful feather head-dresses?"

"Let's go up to the studio, Duchess," I said, gathering the printed matter, "where we can look at these things in comfort; we'll have a session."

"The very thing," she replied; "then you can unpack your fishing rod."

"What do you mean?" I asked. "Have you bought me a fishing rod?"

"Yes, I thought you really ought to have a good one, Dan," she said, "so I stopped in at Scaler and Pike's (isn't it funny how often people's names are tied up with what they do?) and I picked out a rod that looked nice to me." I had an awful sinking feeling inside.

"Did you talk with anyone who understood about fishing?" I asked. "Your idea of a rod, Duchess, is that it's something convenient to hang neckties on."

"Why you brute!" she exclaimed, laughing. "Of course, I called in all the experts in the store, and then I bought you the best I could afford."

"And mighty nice of you, too; I'm all excited to see the rod. Come along, Duchess," I said, and together we strolled through the garden, up the steps, and on, into the cool, high-ceiled studio.

"It's a beauty, Duchess," I said when, after unpacking the fishing rod, I had looked it over. "Nicest one I ever had. You're a good scout. Now we'll certainly have to go some place where I can use it catching trout." Pleased that I liked her present, the Duchess pushed aside the things on the old Spanish tavern table (the one I bought at an auction for nine dollars!) and on its wide top of chestnut wood we spread out the maps she had brought from New York—of Canada's prairie provinces, of Alberta and of British Columbia.

Having got a sort of bird's-eye impression of the area between Montreal and Banff, we next looked through all the folders.

"Duchess," I said, "having recently agreed that there would be no sense in anyone leaving a place like this, where would you rather be in July and August?"

Smiling, the Duchess answered briskly:

"In Banff, for the big trail ride on July thirtieth. And you, Dan?"

"I'd enjoy the ride, too; a lake where I could get in a lick with this new rod would suit me better; but if we should go all the way to Banff I should want to start in time to see the Stampede at Calgary. That begins on July fifth, according to this—" and I held up a folder. "I happen to know it is the biggest rodeo in the country; many prize-winning riders of our Western States go up to Calgary for Stampede Week."

"Here's a time-table," said the Duchess, flipping over a page, "which shows that from Montreal to Banff, where the trail ride starts, is twenty-three hundred miles. It takes a train more than two and a half days to make the trip." Looking at me she continued: "That would be a terribly long trek for Sally; why, her knees would be shaking by the time we had reached high altitudes. She might even fold up entirely."

"Come, now," I said, smiling at the Duchess; "don't let a sudden desire to ride on a railroad train make you underestimate Sally's powers; she's a grand car, and there's a lot of life in the old girl yet, but I grant you she eats a lot of hay—perhaps I should say gas. And she's too big to use off the good roads."

By the end of the session in the studio we had come to the conclusion that because we had never seen the Canadian Rockies we were in a bad way, practically uneducated, and that we owed it to ourselves to do something about it. Also, that if one were going as far as 2,300 miles, one would save money to make it 2,900 and get the whole thing, right out to the Pacific Ocean. And, finally, that the really sensible thing to do in our case would be to make a summer of it, June to October, and see the Canadian West as it should be seen.

"What was the name of the strange man who wrote you the letter, Duchess, that sent you up into the attic, that made you open a trunk and put on the old boots?"

The Duchess went off into a peal of laughter, as she said: "You'd never guess, Dan. It was *Acorn!*"

CHAPTER II

WITH SALLY TO MONTREAL

MONDAY, the twenty-eighth of June, I tossed sixteen pieces of luggage into the tonneau of our old and faithful motor-car, Sally.

"It's indecent to have so many things," exclaimed the Duchess, who was standing by as I worked; "but what can one do, with three months' travel ahead, that will bring changing temperatures and all kinds of activities?"

"To say nothing of social affairs, and tea fights," I added, placing a lunch basket on top of the load, where it could be easily reached.

"Really, Dan, if I thought all this luggage would be tagging along with us wherever we go this summer, I'd give up, right now."

"Get into your seat, Duchess," I said as I climbed into mine; "we can cache groups of bags along the route and pick them up on the way back."

"That's a lovely idea," she exclaimed, laughing till she got me going too. "Your pyjamas would always be at one place when you and your razor were at another!

And to think," she went on, "that all this scheme for a fancy summer came out of an old pair of boots!"

With Sally heading for Canada, I let in the clutch, and drove away from the door of our Connecticut home at half past eight in the morning.

All that day the weather was grey, to rain, but everything was fine with us as we rode along U.S. Route 7, through the beautiful country of Connecticut, Massachusetts, and Vermont. The basket packed with lunch and thermos bottles of hot coffee gave us the fun of eating out of doors and saved time. In eleven hours we were settled for the night in a good cabin near Burlington, Vermont.

The next morning skies were clearing when, having breakfasted and stowed the overnight bags, we set out upon the short lap to Montreal. A crowd of tourists at the Canadian Border Customs House near Swanton delayed us twenty minutes.

It was sunny high noon when we drove into Montreal. The Duchess began to look excited.

"What a fine city it is!" I said, waving a hand toward the trees that embowered the streets. "It's good to be back here again."

"Let's gather the clan for tea at the Ritz this afternoon. What do you say, Dan?" asked the Duchess, with her mind all made up.

"Right, oh!" I answered; "nothing would suit me better. There's a telephone in that drug store on the next corner," and I pulled Sally up to the curb. "Try to get Clifford Wilson."

"Surely, and Louise Bowman and Hilda Turner. But aren't you going to get out and run around? Aren't you excited to be in Montreal?" asked the Duchess, hopping out herself.

"Go ahead," I answered. "I'll wait for you here; I'm getting my excitement through the eye."

The tea fight that afternoon ramified in every direction like ripples from a stone flung into a pool; and every ripple was edged with laughter. Tea turned into dinner, dinner into a theatre party and the theatre party ended as a midnight supper.

Late the next afternoon, Wednesday, June 30, the Duchess and I had a big time at the Canadian Pacific Station, attending to luggage, and when this job was finished I noticed she looked in need of a bracer. Suggesting that we dine early, I took her to the Mount Royal Hotel. Food always works a miracle on the Duchess, reviving her as water revives a wilted plant, and this time was no exception.

We were lingering over the coffee when suddenly she exclaimed:

"How stupid of me! I haven't bought a bit of dried fruit to take with us. How can one go trail riding without an emergency ration of fruit?"

"To hear you," I answered, "one would suppose forest rangers always carry raisins in their pockets."

"They're silly if they don't," she replied, jumping up. "We have more than an hour before the train leaves. Would you mind, Dan, sauntering around? Perhaps there's a grocery store near by." I got up and, as we made our way together through the hotel lobby, the Duchess continued talking:

"Why, it would be almost cosy to get snow-bound in the Rocky Mountains if one had a good stock of dried fruit."

"Yes," I said, "I can see us sitting in an Indian tepee on a shore of Lake Magog, I saying to you, 'Duchess, please pass the figs.'" We burst out laughing as we were passing the dignified doorman of the Mount Royal, and gave him quite a shock.

After a long walk we found what the Duchess so greatly desired, and, with a good-sized package of dried apricots, figs, prunes and raisins under my arm, she and I turned our steps toward the station.

The Park, up the hill from Windsor Station, was empty and tranquil in the light of early evening. We sat down upon one of the benches near the monument. Sparrows were flying about the paths, settling for a moment, then rising again into the quiet air.

"I hope Sally won't be lonely in her storage place," remarked the Duchess. "The poor dear really needs a vacation after all the trips she has taken for us. I shall miss her terribly this summer, but really I'm glad we're going to the Pacific Coast by railroad—it will be something new, travelling by rail, after so much motoring. And you, Dan, will be able to look about you to your heart's content."

"We'd better be moving along to the train," I said, and as we walked down the hill to Windsor Station the Duchess remarked:

"As for me, Dan, all I can think of now is that for two full days and a piece of a third, I shall have nothing to do but eat, sleep, and watch the landscape go by."

The clock in Montreal's Windsor Station showed the time to be seven-thirty, when the Duchess and I, assisted by a cheerful Negro porter, passed through a milling holiday crowd to the gate for the Canadian Pacific crack train, *The Dominion,* bound for Calgary and points west. In one hand I carried the package of dried fruits, and in the other my fishing rod.

As we were being shown to our section in the train, the Duchess laughingly remarked:

"Here we are, travelling on *The Dominion,* the eve of Dominion Day—we couldn't be more Canadian if we tried!"

Neatly stowing our hand luggage, the porter, with a polite bow, left us. The Duchess, with a sigh of contentment, sank into the cushioned seat.

"Air-conditioned car! I shall sleep tonight. What more could one want, Dan, than fresh air—and a sunbeam?"

"A tree?" I suggested, "possibly a river, and a fish," placing my rod carefully in a corner by the window. "And, now that we are moved in and settled for the next sixty-two hours, what do you say, Duchess, to taking a look at the locomotive?"

"I'd love to see what is going to pull us, for Sally's sake and my own. As you may remember, I'm keen about locomotives. We have fifteen minutes before the train leaves; if we hurry we can do it."

There has been a thrill in every railroad train for me since I was a youngster. Now, strolling along a platform of Windsor Station, passing all sorts of men and women who were enacting the drama of departure, I felt an excitement which was shared, I knew, by the Duchess.

"What a creature!" she exclaimed, as we stopped beside the huge driving-wheels of the locomotive. "Sally put next to this would look like a trilobite!" Whether or not the engineer was acquainted with trilobites, I shall never know, but he happened to be leaning out of his cab window and, as he touched his cap to us, I saw an amused smile flicker across his face. Taking for granted that he had heard, the Duchess, looking up at him, continued:

[15]

"Sally is our LaSalle roadster. She is pretty old now and the Cariboo Trail didn't seem quite the thing for an old lady, so we are giving her a rest for the summer in Montreal, and we are going by rail to Vancouver, stopping off here and there along the way. I see your Sally has a number instead of a name: two, eight, one, six. Why don't you call her Rita?" ("There's the Ingersoll streak in the Duchess coming out in a flood of words," I thought to myself.)

"Why, you see, lady," replied the fine-looking engineer, "the largest locomotives used on this railway are the ones whose numbers begin with two, eight. This one —Rita, shall we say?" smiling, "has nineteen sisters."

"My!" exclaimed the Duchess, her eyes opening wide. "Up here in Canada you certainly have large families!" That brought a laugh. Glancing at the clock on his signal board, the engineer nodded to me, saying:

"You'd better get aboard, sir. We'll be pulling out in three minutes."

"I hope I see two, eight, one, six again," said the Duchess, waving a hand toward the man who would be guiding our destiny through part of the night.

We ran down the platform to the nearest pair of steps, and up into a car. A moment later, at exactly 7:50, Standard Time, with scarcely a tremor, *The Dominion* moved out of Montreal Station, and, gathering speed, began her long run to the West.

Settled opposite one another in our comfortable section, the Duchess asked:

"Did you notice his face, Dan? Our engineer is the right sort; he could get us safely across the continent in a dish-pan. Now I shall have a peaceful night's rest, and you too, poor thing"—putting a hand upon my knee—"if you don't roll out of the upper berth." That made me laugh as I was hunting through pockets for my pipe.

"Speaking of the man behind the gun," she remarked, "I don't suppose either of us will ever forget the New York episode involving a penthouse that to us looked like heaven, and its owner who acted as though he had been brought up in hell. It was the experience we had in escaping from the clutches of that creature which taught me to look first at landlords, and afterward at their buildings." Having found my pipe, I got up preparatory to walking back to the observation car for a smoke. Down at the end of our car I saw the custodian of slumbers making up the berths. Chuckling at my thought, I said:

"Duchess, I hope you are satisfied with the appearance of our porter, because we'll be in a bad way, no matter how pleasant our accommodations, if you discover that, underneath his pleasant appearance, the man is really a bandit."

"Go on with you," she exclaimed, "and breathe smoke if you must. I have a good book and shall stay here."

CHAPTER III

CALGARY PARADE

The Duchess's Diary

Saturday night, July 3:—When another engine pulled our long train of cars into Calgary at nine-thirty this morning, completing a run from Montreal Wednesday night of 2,242 miles, *on time,* Dan and I were the first off the train. As I stepped onto the station platform, I looked up and smiled at the wide sky of Canada. Around us was a cheerful bustle of people arriving and departing. The happy-looking Negro porter who was carrying our small luggage to the adjoining Hotel Palliser brought us out into a street filled with sunlight that gilded roofs and towers of the surrounding city. Keeping pace with Dan I said:

"If this sunny expression on the face of things is natural to Calgary, Calgary must be a cheerful place in which to live." And he answered:

"A terrific downpour of rain yesterday is the reason for Calgary's smiles today. You see, Duchess, there have been weeks of drought in this area; I heard two men talking about it just before we got off the train. Thousands of dollars' worth of grass, and crops—and cattle, if it comes to that—have been saved by yesterday's rain. Every ranchman here for the Stampede has a double reason for holiday spirits. And, as the ranches go, so goes Calgary."

"I'd better write a jingle and call it, 'There was gold in that rainy day for me.' " As I said that, there we were, with Dan stepping aside to let me pass through the doorway into the Hotel Palliser.

A pleasing atmosphere enveloped the hotel lobby. After Dan had arranged for a three-day stay in Calgary, we were shown to our apartment and found that its west windows gave us a view of snow-capped Rocky Mountains, and thrillingly beautiful they looked. (Later the roof garden gave us an even finer view.) The big tub I saw through the bath-room door looked marvellous to me after the cold cream and alcohol rubs of the train trip. It didn't take us long to get into fresh things, and then out we went to see the town.

Calgary was bright and busy. In the course of our rambles we visited Eaton's and the Hudson's Bay Company's fine department stores. In the latter Dan made a bee-line for the section devoted to equipment for fishermen. While he was getting himself hooked, and all tied up in lines, I made what might be called a humming-bird flight to the book department. (I've read that humming-birds fly across the Gulf of Mexico in one night!) Mr. Hunter, head of the book department, happened at that moment to be out, but Miss Borrowman, in charge, helped me to get quickly what I wanted. Rejoined Dan, and together we visited the public library. Mr. Alexander Calhoun, librarian, took us to his office for a chat. He, it seems, is an authority on the Rocky Mountains, and when we told him our plans he gave us an introduction to the Alpine Club in Banff, our next stopping place, and also an invitation to go with the members of the club on their annual encampment, which this summer is to be in Little Yoho Valley.

Today after luncheon Dan expressed a desire to see the creatures at the Zoo on St. George's Island, so I went along with him to 12th Street East, and we enjoyed seeing a variety of wild animals and birds. Later we drove out to Bowness Park, about eight miles west of the city. The highway leading to the Park runs parallel to the Bow River. It's amusing that there is also an Elbow River here, and sixty odd years ago where these two mountain streams join, at Calgary (the Gaelic name for "clear running water"), a detachment of Royal Northwest Mounted Police built a fort. Those "Mounties" little knew what they were starting—the foundations of the largest city in the Province of Alberta.

Driving back from Bowness Park, Dan told me of the irrigation project immediately east of Calgary devel-

Indian River.

oped by the Canadian Pacific Railway. On both sides of the track for 140 miles the land is irrigated by water from the Bow River. The entire block of land consists of 3,000,000 acres, a nice little parcel. Most of it will ultimately be brought under irrigation.

This is a great ranching and stock-raising country, and for thousands of square miles (everything is large scale in Canada) the grass for grazing is particularly nutritious.

Sunday, the Fourth of July:—Considering a certain famous day in 1776, it is amusing that Dan and I celebrated the anniversary of American Independence by attending the eight o'clock service in the English church, Calgary's Pro-Cathedral; which is another way of saying that Christianity is bigger than national boundaries. Knowing the Cathedral was but a few blocks from the hotel, we decided to walk. Dan's bump of location that he is so proud of played him false; he made a wrong turn and we almost crossed the Canadian boundary into the States before we finally discovered the church we were seeking.

After service, and a substantial breakfast, we drove in a taxi to the Calgary Golf and Country Club, where I now am writing. I couldn't help thinking of dear old Sally—in a loft in Montreal. But I really am glad that on this, our first trip through Western Canada, Dan

will be free to gaze as much as he likes upon the won-
drous scenes that will lie about us, and will not have to
keep his eye glued to the road. Of course I should not
feel this way if the Canadian Pacific Railway did not
run through the most beautiful country, and if it did
not have open observation cars.

It is eleven o'clock. Dan and his fellow players of the
ancient game have disappeared from my field of vision
as I sit in the shade of blossoming lilacs; air like wine is
stirring the leafage of silver birches that march in close
formation each side of the club's private driveway up
the distant hill to a wide and cloudless blue sky. . . .

Noontide:—I have been watching players come hurrying down the hillside, big men striding free, and small
boys lugging their bags of heavy "irons"; a sight as re-
pulsive to me as a fox-hunt. They finish where a little
flag is flying on the smooth green near the club-house.

One o'clock:—Here comes Dan, and about time, too.
I've read everything within reach. He is walking cheerfully, as though the sunshine were not hot enough to
fry eggs. I'm glad Dan picked a husky-looking caddy.
We're having luncheon here, so, no more diary now.

Later, Sunday night, July 4:—At four o'clock Mr.
Hunter, the man of books, called at the Palliser Hotel
and drove us to his home, he and Mrs. Hunter having
invited us to tea. It was delightful to find ourselves
among friendly young people on this Sunday afternoon.

Dan and I love tea parties. This one started indoors, and then settled down in a shady spot on the lawn. As guests drifted across the grass, chairs for them were added to the circle already around the tea table. Among others, besides the Hunters themselves, with whom I enjoyed talking, were Jean and Tony Drew, and Muriel and Hugh Inksater.

Muriel Wright (the professional name of Mrs. Inksater) is in charge of the CFAC Radio Station in the Southam Building, and she has asked me to broadcast at four o'clock Monday, tomorrow, afternoon. I said I would, not till later recalling that the opening program of the Stampede will be in full swing about that time. Shall I miss the Wild Cow Milking?

Monday, July 5:—Calgary was aflutter on this opening day of the Stampede when Dan and I, after breakfast, took a twenty-minute walk around town. Folks young and old in holiday attire were hurrying along to get places on the line of march of the big Parade due to pass our hotel about ten-thirty o'clock.

The lobby of the Palliser when we returned was full of ranchmen and cowboys, in broad-brimmed hats and chaps; other picturesque figures were scattered among a crowd that was laughing and talking. Making our way through to the elevators, Dan and I went up to the second floor where certain front windows had been reserved for guests of the hotel. By this time the sun of early morning had disappeared under clouds, and the air was cold. I was delighted that we would be able to watch the whole show as it passed, protected from wind and possible rain.

Parade Notes:

10:30 A. M.:—Police Motor Cycle Squad appears. Through the open windows in front of us all the persons in our group look out upon the crowd in the street below and hear them shout: "They're coming!" A gentleman on my left, seeing me writing, and realizing that I am a stranger offers to give me the names of persons in the pageant. I thank him, nodding a yes, as the Parade Marshal's car appears in the street below. ("That's James Smart," I'm told—"pioneer fire chief."), followed by Sergeant Buchanan and eight red-coated Royal Canadian Police constables. Now the parade is really on, for here comes a massed band—Elks, Shriners, and Calgary Regimental, marching along and filling the air with stirring music. . . . Hurrah! . . . Cars, in which ride officials, and dignitaries of the Federal and Provincial Governments pass along; they are followed by a detachment of the Strathcona's Horse, commanded by Lieutenant Colonel Devey, and eight troopers in khaki and Stetson hats (these were organized in the Boer War). I notice that four of their beautiful horses have black tails and four have bay, a nice touch. . . .

Another detachment comes marching—these in blue breeches, red tunics, and plumed brass helmets, pre-war dress uniforms. How gay, and at the same time how archaic they look! . . . Now, men in khaki serge and tin hats appear and bring with them a sudden sharp thrust of remembrance. The crowd breaks into cheering. . . . They are followed by men in summer uniforms and sun helmets.

Dan and I are all worked up and cheering with the best of them. Suddenly, swinging along down the middle of the street comes Jumbo, a man-power elephant, winning laughter and applause. . . . Noise from the crowd below in the street makes me get up for a better look, and at the same instant we hear, and see, that "The Indians are coming!"

Blackfoot Indians from Gleichen, handsome creatures, splendid in embroidered white buck-skin, and wearing beautiful feather head-dresses (war bonnets, really—on this peaceful day). They are riding by on white, bay or pinto "ponies" (the cayuse, or small Indian horse). My neighbour on the left whispers that these Indians are wealthy and prosperous. They are followed by the Blackfoot Tribal Band from Browning, Montana. . . .

Here come the Sarcee Indians, who, I am told, live near Calgary; they are led by Chief Jo Big Plume! (I think I shall call Dan Chief Dan No Hat!). . . . Hurrah! Another band, the Stony Indians from their Reservation at Morley (we shall pass Morley on our way to Banff). Fine looking men they are, too. The Stonys are led by Chief David Bearspaw. (He and a bear must have shaken hands on an important occasion!) Dan, on my right, whispers, "Hey, Duchess, take a look at the squaws." Of course I'm looking at the Indian squaws as they come by riding the travois, at the end of their section, with immobile faces, their solemn-eyed papooses strapped to their shoulders. I visualize all their hard work (imagine a lifetime of camping!) caring for their children, making and embroidering their husband's costumes (as well as their own); and what they get is the end of the line, while the coats they embroidered are up in front. I stand and shout: "Hurrah for the Squaws! Hurrah for the Papooses!" till Dan pulls me down into my seat.

"Well, look at them," I exclaim. "Did you ever see better sports? In the midst of all this noise and excitement not one of those babies is whimpering, and the mothers are doing their stuff without batting an eye!"

"It's time you had food," Dan remarks.

"We can't go yet," I answer; "here come the floats. Look! A big globe—the Hudson's Bay Company, and on it the words: 'We search the world to satisfy your needs.'"

"My need at this moment," said Dan, "is for a juicy steak, and if we don't get to the dining-room before the mob, we'll have a long wait and miss the opening of the Stampede at Victoria Park."

"Hold on for another few minutes," I urge Dan. . . . Cowboys, wearing red shirts, riding horses, or sitting in farm wagons and yelling wildly, pass by. (There's a

prize for the "outfit" that makes the most noise!) I should think they'd all get prizes!

"That's David Luxa, a patriarch of this country," says my neighbour on the left, indicating a man riding in an ancient wagon, holding a muzzle-loader in his hands. "Watch the string of old conveyances that are following him, filled with members of his family. Luxa has taken first, second and third prizes for this exhibit. He's got the prizes on his gun barrel." I am amused to see an old "Surrey" among the Red River carts, and Prairie Schooners. . . . Ranchmen playing mandolins atop a loaded wagon, sing as they pass, and behind them are riders from Red Top, Wyoming.

The Native Boys' Band of Calgary, wearing red and white capes and blue trousers, march by dispensing music. . . . Oxen hitched to a covered wagon. . . . The Bagpipers of Drumheiler— Oh, I wouldn't have missed these Scottish laddies for anything; they are wearing blue coats, blue and green plaid kilts, with a dash of red here and there, and white leggings. The crowd goes wild at the sight and sound of them. . . . Now a covered wagon drawn by horses goes slowly along, and I notice its wheels look as though they would love to come off. . . . The Calgary Sea Cadets—sailor boys in blue, with white capes; we give them a hand. . . . More Highlanders, and cheers; they are a grand lot of men representing four or five clans. . . . S.P.C.A. exhibit— splendidly groomed horses. . . . West Canadian Colliery exhibit—an enormous block of coal. . . . Six grand Percherons wearing red blankets advertise Beau's bacon. This is too suggestive to a hungry man, and Dan gets up. I follow . . . and we head for the elevators.

CHAPTER IV

STAMPEDE

As the Duchess and I stepped out of the elevator, we saw that the lobby of the Palliser was crowded, jammed. Cowboys and cowgirls, real ones, some of whom would take part in the Stampede later; others who wanted to look like the real thing, wearing ten-gallon hats and bright scarfs around their necks.

Passing the news-stand I grabbed a copy of the Calgary *Herald*, and we read a head band across the top of the front page: EARHART CALLS FOR HELP AS SHIPS RACE TO AID.

"Golly, I hope they reach her in time," exclaimed the Duchess; "everything is racing today."

At that moment the Honourable J. C. Bowen, Lieutenant Governor of Alberta, entered the lobby wearing formal morning dress and a grey "topper," officers in snappy uniforms in attendance, and he at once became the centre of a group of friends and admirers. As the Duchess and I pushed through the crowd, it was "Hi, Jim!" and a slap on the back here, and "Hello, Bill! How are things?" there. Everybody friendly and everybody having a good time. I knew they had come from all parts of Canada and the Western States for this annual jamboree—men from the plains who hadn't seen a good crop in three years, mountain men who ran dude ranches, all hoping this would be the best season ever. They had brought teams and chuck wagons, and race-horses for the many events. (Three hundred racehorses arrived from Winnipeg by train last night.) Now, here was the great day!

We met many of the picturesque figures, thanks to the kindness of the hotel manager. One in particular I remember. He was a huge man and, taking the Duchess's hand in his great paw, he said:

"Well, ma'am, we're right glad to see you out here. So this is Dan! I didn't know they made 'em so big in the East." And giving me a slap on the back that set my six feet six rocking, he roared with laughter; then, catching sight of a newly arrived rancher as big as himself, he said, "Excuse me, ma'am," and rushed off.

"Hi, Jim," we heard, and another roar of laughter, as he gave his friend a smack on the back.

"I'm pretty well shaken down, Duchess," I said as we slid into the dining-room; "how about you?"

"Luncheon is going to cost you twice as much as it would have an hour ago," she replied as the head waiter seated us at a pleasant table for two.

[30]

1:30 P. M.:—"How gay it is, Dan, with the flags flying and the crowds milling around," said the Duchess, as, taxi paid off, we passed through an entrance to the Exhibition Grounds of Victoria Park.

The Midway was ablare with brassy music, yelling, and shouting, flags flying and banners blowing in the breeze. Barkers, outside booths and enclosures, implored the passing throng to stop and see something more stupendous than was ever seen before, calling out at the top of their lungs that this was so, or "your money back." We passed "Snack Bars" along the way where everything that could be fried was being fried, filling the air with an acrid smell; and tents where everything that could be coated with sugar was being so coated, and handed to customers, dripping sweetness. Tents where cold things were served "ice cold" and hot things "red hot."

The Duchess and I tossed rings for things we hoped we would not win, took chances on a Wheel of Fortune that gave the holder of the lucky number anything from a rubber doll to a china tea set, and stood for a moment to see what others won.

"Number seven," shouted the attendant, and an Indian squaw with her papoose strapped to her back stepped forward and received a gaudy lamp-shade. "Fine thing for your tepee," said the man as he handed the shade to the pleased and puzzled squaw. Going along again, we came upon huge tractors that were guaranteed to plough up the whole of the Northwest in a single day. Then, automobiles, art exhibits, all sorts of home industries.

When we'd finally reached the promenade in front of the grand stand the Duchess said: "I am memorizing the pattern of the turns we've made in getting here, Dan, so I won't go astray on my way out at three-thirty for the broadcasting. All the right turns will then be left ones, and all the entrances exits—and merely because I shall be looking the other way."

"Don't you begin to philosophize now, Duchess," I said as we settled ourselves in seats that gave us a good view of the brown curving race-track, its whitewashed fences and the oval of trampled turf which they en-closed, today's arena; "before long you'll have plenty of material for that kind of thing given to you free."

"Well, bring it on," she replied smiling. "I'm set for excitement, but I wish the sun were out." The grey sky was heavy with clouds.

"There will be dirty work at the cross-roads," I said "over there near the judges' stand, if it rains this after-noon."

We were looking at our programs when suddenly the loud speaker near us blared forth (Mr. Charles Yule, president of the Stampede, was speaking.): "Pete

Knight, one of the world's greatest riders, a champion of Calgary Stampede three times, a champion of North America three times and three times champion rider of the world, was trampled to death by a wild horse on May twenty-third of this year, at Hayward, California. We will observe one minute of silence in his memory." The crowd rose to its feet. . . . The Duchess, without speaking, held toward me a postcard she had bought on the way in; it carried a picture of Pete Knight sitting with ease and grace on the curved back of a bucking horse. . . .

"Golly," exclaimed the Duchess as we sat down again, "that must make the boys who are waiting to do their stuff feel cheerful. To pit a man, no matter how brave and strong, against a wild horse seems to me as sensible as to test a fine watch by throwing it against a stone wall."

The loud speaker continued to pour out words. Mr. Yule was now introducing the Honourable J. G. Gardiner, of Ottawa, Federal Minister of Agriculture, who arose and said:

"On behalf of the Government of Canada and the people of Canada who look to this exhibition as giving an inspiration toward higher quality in live-stock and agriculture in the Dominion, it gives me great pleasure to pronounce it officially open."

The great rodeo was on! A look at our programs

showed that during the afternoon Canadian and North
American champion riders would compete for prizes in:

> Bucking Horse Riding
> Bareback Bucking Horse Riding
> Calf Roping
> Wild Steer Bareback Riding
> Wild Steer Decorating
> Wild Cow Milking
> Wild Horse Racing
> Indian Horse Racing

The Duchess ran her eye down this list of events for
the afternoon and exclaimed:

"There's not a chance of my seeing the Wild Cow
Milking. It will come too late; but if I miss seeing some
bones broken I shan't mind."

On a big platform exposed to the weather, out in
front, a high school band struck up a smashing march.
By the time the number was finished, a drizzling rain
was falling and, picking up their instruments, the young
players made a dash for the grand stand to save their
white uniforms. From loud speakers came announce-
ment of the first contest.

Watching eagerly we saw men in attendance at the
gate of the corral jump aside as it opened upon the
arena, and out shot a wild and lunging horse. Cheers
went up from the crowded stand for the man on his
back. Once, twice, three times the horse jumped high,

back arched, landing on legs stiff as steel, his rider clinging. The fourth time the horse's feet struck the earth,
his rider struck it also; and, picking himself up, he
limped off the field.

Four more contestants, one after the other, tried their
luck in the muddy arena, and all were thrown off by
their plunging beasts.

Rain was by now blowing in upon the forward seats
of the grand stand. With a lot of others the Duchess and
I scurried up to higher seats where the roof gave protec-
tion. But we and the crowd forgot all about the rain
when Nick Knight, of Cody, Wyoming, came out of the
chute on Old Man River, a big grey that humped his
back and thrashed around in the mud trying to get rid
of Knight; but Knight stuck to him and, amid great
applause, won the day's prize money for this event.

"Ladies and gentlemen," blared the loud speakers,
"the calf roping contest is about to begin. Champions of
Canada and the United States will compete. The calf in
each instance is to be roped, thrown and tied. Prize
money for the shortest time."

"I shall like this," exclaimed the Duchess. "There
ought not to be any bones involved." My acquaintance
with calves was merely the picturesque one of seeing
them with their mothers in a green pasture, so I was all
interest.

The champion calf roper of Canada was announced

and, looking, we saw him on his horse, ready beside the chute, rope in hand.

The gate of the chute opened, and out shot a brown and white streak of lightning.

The cowboy instantly started in pursuit, holding his coiled rope; at the right moment he cast it ahead of the sprinting calf, and I thought, "How skilful," as the noose opened in just the right way to settle around the calf's neck; but something missed, because the calf ran right through the noose and continued to beat it.

A roar went up from the spectators. Our champion now dug his spurs into his horse and thundered down the field, again casting his rope ahead of the calf. As the rope flashed out this time, the crowd began cheering for the calf. Bravely the little fellow kept on toward freedom, and, if you'll believe it, he loped through the noose again. Forgotten, now, was the champion; the shouts of the crowd were all for the gay little calf that, with a fling of its hind quarters, disappeared into the runway at the end of the arena.

Yes, the calves gave the crowd a great laugh, for three of them in turn romped right through the noose, each time the cowboys "slid the ropes" over them, swishing their tails happily as they ran. A man named Clark Lund, however, showed us all how it should be done; he snared his calf at the west end of the field and had him tied in a bundle before one could count ten. There was

Going up the Indian River

another shout from the crowd when a calf that had
been roped ran playfully around the horse, and finally
got between the cowboy's legs and carried him down
the field.

Now, a cowboy's horse went thundering after a calf;
his rope sailed out, his trained horse seemed actually to
sit down, bracing his front feet, and instantly at the
end of the rope the calf was brought up short, doing a
wild dance. Off his horse in a second the cowboy rushed
to the little creature, threw it on its side and, with lightning passes of the rope, tied its feet together. Then he
jumped to his feet and held up his hand. At this signal a
judge rode up, examined the knot, then raised *his* hand.
The loud speaker announced:

"Nine and one fifth seconds."

"Incredible!" exclaimed the Duchess.

In the bareback steer riding contest each rider, having
succeeded in getting astride his big steer, held on by one
hand to a rope that had been placed around its body
just back of the front legs. We had thought the horses
full of action, but, when the first steer came out of the
chute, his technique made the horses look tame. He
jumped, head down, forelegs braced, and flung his hind
quarters to the right; jumped and flung his hind quarters
to the left. The circular motion plus the downward
plunge four times put his rider in the mud. The steers
seemed to delight in the wetness, and spoiled a lot of

bright-coloured shirts by throwing their riders.

We were excited when a big black steer came plunging into the arena, throwing himself all over it in his fight to dislodge his rider. The cowboy stuck to him, holding one hand in the air all the time, unbelievable as it seems, until the time was up and he had won the contest. A roar of applause went up from the crowd.

Just as the Wild Steer Decorating contest began, I saw the Duchess look at her watch.

"Wait a minute," I urged. "You've time to see this; it ought to be interesting." And so it proved to be. Steers were released at the west end of the paddock, and cowboys on their horses chased them madly up the field; when close enough they swung themselves off their horses onto the steers and then tried to place a decoration on one of the steer's wide horns. Herman Linder, many times the "all-round" champion cowboy rider, got hurt in this contest, when the steer he was on threw its head around and flung Linder off. He landed on his knee and was led out of the arena limping.

"Oh, I hope he isn't badly injured," exclaimed the Duchess. "Knees are such horrid things to hurt. Well, that's enough for me, Dan; get me out of this quickly, I've exactly time to reach the broadcasting station."

As the Duchess whirled away in a taxi from an exit of Victoria Park, she called back to me:

"Mind the wild cows!"

CHAPTER V

CHUCK WAGONS AND FIREWORKS

AGAIN in my grand stand seat, I saw that the arena was set for the milking. Down at the west end thirty or forty wild cows were stirring around, while at the east end of the oval as many cowboys, seated on their horses, were waiting the word to "go." Time was the factor in this event. The men would work in teams—one man to select the cow and rope her, his partner to do the milking. The quickest team would win the prize money. Every milker carried a quart bottle.

I knew I couldn't watch all at the same time, so I singled out a likely looking pair of "boys" and determined to keep my eyes glued to them.

The judge in his box raised the red flag, then dropped it; the contest in wild cow milking was on.

Down the field went the cowboys. The rushing of their horses sounded like distant thunder; it was the charge of another kind of Light Brigade. Sods flew from the horses' hoofs as they tore along bearing down on the alarmed cows.

My pair of "boys" were among those in the front

ranks. Suddenly I saw a cow, frightened by the approaching riders, break away from the milling herd. My two boys saw, and seized their opportunity; they veered to one side, letting the crowding riders pass. Then I saw one of them throw a rope into the air, saw its noose settle around the insurgent cow's neck. In a second she was roped tight to the rider's saddle. The other fellow, off his horse in a second, rushed frantically to the caught beast to do his stuff.

There was nothing orthodox in the way this milker went about getting the milk into his bottle. The cow, held tight by the head, was flouncing the rest of herself around in circles. Watching his chance as the cow came near, the would-be milker grabbed her tail and with a quick motion wound it around his neck, tucking the end under his chin. Then, with head bent, both hands free, he dug his heels into the ground and went in the back way, so to speak—between her legs and stamping hoofs. In less than no time at all I saw the milker release the cow's tail, run swiftly to the judge's stand, holding up in his bottle what from my distance looked a half pint of milk.

The arena, while this act was going on, was a scene of confusion, a general mixup, in which the cows were pulling cowboys all over the muddy lot at the ends of their ropes, or cows uncaught were plunging around, knocking over milkers who were about to succeed in getting what they wanted. There wasn't a cow in the picture that by any stretch of the imagination could have been called contented.

When the Duchess returned to the grand stand she told me of excitement at the radio station. An electric storm in the vicinity of Calgary had all but stopped the broadcasting. The Duchess said:

"Muriel Wright, the director of station CFAC, watched the dials and the hands of the big clock anxiously. I was to go on the air at four o'clock. At three minutes before the hour there was a clearing of conditions, and when the hour struck she and I went into our 'interview' and continued for the fifteen minutes without hindrance. It was the first time," said the Duchess, "that I ever broadcast without 'copy,' but all went well. Miss Wright is clever in getting people to talk naturally. And now, what has happened here?"

"Milking wild cows is no job for a pretty maid, Duchess," I said. "It is just as well you were not present at the contest; you would have felt bad to see so many gay shirts thrown into the mud along with their wearers. And as for the milk, you could have put it all into a pint bottle."

When the Indian horse race was finished we left the grand stand and hunted for a place to eat.

"There it is," cried the Duchess as we were walking along the Midway, and I too saw the big tent she indicated. It was filled with tables at which many were already eating their dinners. The Ladies' Aid Societies of several Calgary churches ran this restaurant during Stampede week; we had been told the dinner would be good, and it was that.

"Eat hearty, my lad," urged the Duchess. "If we are going to see this opening day of the Stampede through to the finish, we shall need all the food they will give us here. Our emotions have a lot ahead of them if they only knew it." I laid my program on the table and, as I ate, looked at the evening events.

"Chuck wagon races at seven-thirty," I read. "They will be the high spot of the evening. Many of the 'outfits' have travelled a long way to get here, and each of them will have a lot of friends rooting for them. And right after the chuck wagon races comes a cowboy yelling contest. And after that a big stage show, and after that fireworks. Tell me, Duchess," I asked, "when did we start? Is this yesterday or tomorrow?"

"It will be tomorrow before we get back to the Palliser," she replied. "Let's ask for another cup of coffee, Dan, and possibly, another piece of pie."

I began crooning: "Pie, ay, ay, pie, ay, ay," till a passing waitress hearing my song hastened with a smile to bring us coffee and two more golden brown wedges of America's favourite dessert. When we went out of what I might call the Bedouin restaurant (it being in a tent) the Duchess and I felt prepared to face anything.

The arena was all set for the chuck wagon races when we again reached the grand stand.

"Well of all things!" the Duchess exclaimed laughingly, looking at our seats, "here are the old fireside chairs! Pretty soon, Dan, we'll have to see about getting them re-upholstered!" A blare from the loud speakers prevented further badinage.

"Ladies and gentlemen, the first chuck wagon race is about to begin!" Great applause from a fresh crowd that packed the big stand and overflowed into surrounding spaces. The announcer then went on to explain that the four horses hitched to each chuck wagon would be driven by one man; that two outriders would accompany each wagon, their business being, upon the signal, to load the stove and its canvas awning from the ground into a sling at the end of the wagon, remount, and ride with their outfit around the white barrels now placed in the arena (we saw them). Each outfit, after having made the turns around the barrels and reached the race-track, would drive straight to the half-mile post. A prize for doing this in the shortest time would be awarded after the final race Saturday night.

"It takes men to invent a game like that," exclaimed the Duchess. "No woman would call a chuck wagon race fun."

"You'll be excited before this is over," I answered.

[43]

The first and second races were amusing and taught us the technique of the thing. The last outfit in place for the second race made the fastest time, 1 minute and 21 seconds, the driver, a man by the name of Marshall, being the winner. At the end of this race a lost child was taken up to the judges' stand and shown to the audience.

In the third race the wagon marked *Red Top* jerked forward and lost its stove, which fell to the ground. Instantly an outrider picked up the cast iron thing and, holding it under one arm, to the amusement of the crowd, rode valiantly in pursuit of his wagon, but never succeeded in catching up with it. At this time when all were intent upon the outcome of the race, the lost child was claimed by its mother—to the Duchess's great content.

Dick Swan's outfit from Jasper won the third race; his time was 1 minute and 20 seconds.

The fourth chuck wagon race was about to begin. Four outfits were taking their places in the arena. On the top of each wagon was painted the name of the outfit and a number; in the case of this race, 1, 2, 3, and 4. The same procedure was followed in every race. A judge rode around each outfit, looked to see that the stove on the ground was at the right distance from the back of the wagon, and that the awning over the stove was firmly staked.

In this particular race we were attracted to outfit No. 4 because of its fine black horses. Now across the distance we heard the judge call, "All set?"

Back came the cowboys' answer, "Right!"

The red flag at the judges' stand dropped. Four whips cracked out like pistol shots, and the race was on.

No. 4 outfit was leading the other three. The swaying chuck wagon and its four galloping horses made the turn around the first barrel safely, and was approaching the turn around the second, which would have completed the figure eight, when suddenly hell broke loose. The horses had swung around into the race-track too soon, and struck the barrel instead of passing it. Instantly all four of them were thrown to the ground, the wagon turned completely over and, as the crowd in the grand stand rose to its feet in dismay at the sound of the crashing impact, all that remained of Outfit No. 4 was a welter of horses tangled in harness amidst an indescribable heap of debris.

But that wasn't all, for thundering down the track at the same moment, so fast it couldn't stop, and heading straight for that heap of wreckage, came Outfit No. 3.

"Oh, Heavens!" cried the Duchess, almost in tears, and I caught my breath. With our eyes popping out of our heads we saw the four horses and swaying wagon pass clean over prostrate Outfit No. 4 and, still right side up, keep on going to the goal post. Outfits Nos. 1 and 2 managed to veer to one side of the wreck and passed on to the post without accident.

"And to think that everyone was so happy a moment ago!"

"It looks like half a dozen funerals to me," I answered, as we watched men thronging to clear the track. Suddenly the loud speaker sounded and everyone held still to catch the words:

"Ladies and gentlemen: The Management is glad to announce that no one in Outfit Number Four was injured and no horses were hurt."

"Hurrah!" from the grand stand. I grabbed the Duchess by the shoulders and shook her till she squealed with laughter. The announcer continued:

"The winner of the chuck wagon race is Dick Cosgrave, of Outfit Number Three." Cheers. "The time: One minute, seventeen and four-fifths seconds."

"The whole thing is *unbelievable,*" said the Duchess. "I'm glad the yelling contest comes next. Watch out, for I'm going to yell my head off."

The cowboy events were finished for the day a little after eight o'clock, standard time. In the long Western evening, sun was still shining upon the scene around us as the Duchess and I sat among hundreds of spectators in Victoria Park grand stand watching below us a moving mass of ranchmen and their friends, all talking and laughing, who filled the space between us and the stage with a sea of felt hats and bright coloured handker-chiefs.

There were groups of Indian women and children in the crowd, as well as fine looking "braves," who kept more or less to the east end of the promenade. One Indian in particular drew my attention—tall and slim, with aquiline features, black hair hanging in two braids on each side of his face, its character increased by the shadow of a wide-brimmed black Stetson hat. He was wearing an emerald-green shirt that turned him into a figure of romance.

The strain of contests over, everyone was out for a good time, eager for the stage show. To the Duchess's great delight, and mine, about 8:30 preparations began for the Cavalcade of Hits.

The big platform, which had been used all day for speakers and bands, was turned, as we watched, into a stage. Scenery, piece by piece, was set up, enclosing it in pseudo-oriental splendour. The sky itself became the proscenium arch. A house on wheels for use as dressing rooms was drawn close to the back of the stage.

Sitting there in the bright evening while golden clouds of sunset floated in stillness upon a sky of serene blue, we saw fantasy being built before our eyes. Suddenly the Duchess leaned toward me and said in low tones:

"Look toward the east end. Do you see the group of

Indians standing by themselves—the young father holding his baby so tenderly, and the mother, who is probably tired, and the two tiny boys standing beside her,
silent and bewildered under their big wide black felt
hats? I wish there was a place for them to sit down.
They are looking eagerly toward the stage, I wish they
could sit down and see the whole show in comfort."

I was touched, too, by the sight of that Indian family.
At intervals during the next hour, whenever I happened to turn my head in their direction, I saw the hat-
less and coatless father and mother, with their three children, standing motionless, gazing with what seemed
absorbed eagerness at the stage lights and storied brilliance
so magically created by the white man.

Suddenly the stage lights shone forth; the Cavalcade
of Hits was on. As snappy music, clever skits, humor-
ous sketches, strikingly costumed and beautifully performed ballets succeeded one another, actors and audience seemed caught up by pleasure into a bond of good
fellowship. Everybody was happy. The program would
have been good in any theatre; the fact that it was out
of doors, on a perfect evening, gave it a charm that lin-
gers with me still.

In the seats directly below us a big bear of a man and
the plain little woman beside him watched intently a
faery-like ballet—girlish forms in delicate costumes
dancing to the rhythm of the song:

[48]

"It's raining vi-o-lets,"
while they twirled parasols circled with electric lights.
With the second verse of the song, emotion overcame
the man, and his arm stole around his companion. The
Duchess didn't miss this, and whispered to me, "Beauty's
power to bind."

The whole crowd were happily bound together when
the program came to a brilliant end. Then, even as it had
been built up, piece by piece, the scenery was taken
down and removed. Finally the house on wheels seemed
of itself to move off mysteriously into the gathering
darkness.

FIREWORKS

Against the soft gloom long stems of light sprang up
the sky and broke into flower. Silver stars fell out of
dark heavens upon the field of night. Whirling suns
and moons showered loveliness down the sky and suddenly ceased to be.

With flowers of light figuring the curtain of midnight
which hangs between today and tomorrow, the Duchess
and I drove homeward, agreeing that Monday, July
fifth, had been in truth "A great day."

CHAPTER VI

CHOO-CHOO

The Duchess's Diary

July 6, on board C.P.R. train *Dominion*, 9:45 A. M.:—With minds full of the Stampede, Dan and I fell asleep early today (1 A. M.) and slept so late that we had to do a little chuck wagon race of our own to catch this 9:30 A. M. train for Banff. What we did with our large pieces of luggage, when we found there was no time to check them, closely resembled what the cowboys do with their cast iron stoves in a chuck wagon race.

Led by panting porters, Dan and I made a figure eight around invisible white barrels as we tore through the Palliser Hotel lobby, out into the street, into the station and out again onto the platform where a big iron horse stood at the head of a quarter mile of Pullmans, puffing with impatience to depart. Our dusky helpers rushed straight to the nearest car and tossed upon its platform our wild assortment of bags and cases; there was just time to reach them a handful of silver and acknowledge

their grinning good-byes when *The Dominion* began
to slide away from Calgary station.

It is fine on such a blue and golden day to be sitting
out of doors while travelling through beautiful country.
This observation car is built with an open section at
each end and a closed section, mostly glass, in the middle. Indoors or out one can see everything. Dan and I, of
course, are sitting in the open section at the end of the
car, and of the train, which at this moment is skirting
Bow River, running along through wide flat green land
that rises on each side to rolling hills. All is blue above
us; only a few opalescent clouds are to be seen where
hilltops meet the sky.

A beautiful turn in Bow River, and ahead, as the
track curves, glistening snowy mountains are revealed
to us. The river is a peculiar pale cloudy green. We are
in stock-raising country now. On the other bank of the
river I see a group of new ranch buildings. Peeled logs
lie strewn along the river's edge. . . . The Bow makes a
turn and is lost to sight.

10:30 A. M.:—Cochrane—a bright, neat gathering of
low wooden houses, and other buildings, perhaps another
stock ranch. . . . Much of the rolling land we are passing through is smooth as a well-shaved chin; again, other
areas suggest a two days' growth of beard. . . .

Bow River comes back to run under an iron bridge

that our train passes over, and now is on the right side
of us. The track here is single, beautifully ballasted with
the (to me) unique touch of having along each outer
edge of the grey cracked stone a border of white stones
laid mathematically straight. . . .

Mitford—Bow River is running to whiteness at little
rapids. The mountains seem to rise and again sink out of
sight below the horizon line with the curving of the
track. Cirrus clouds hang in the southwestern sky. . . .

The train now is running at about 40 miles an hour
(my guess) up a constantly rising grade; it will have
climbed 1,100 feet by the time we reach Banff. . . .
Sitting out of doors, this way, is delightful. The mountains grow bigger, with weirdly erratic outlines, their
rocky peaks look brittle and crumbly.

Morley Indian Reservation—This is the present-day
home of the Stony Tribe of Indians. Once warlike, they
are now, since their conversion to Christianity by a
saintly missionary, a kindly, industrious and peace-
loving people, noted for the superiority of their bead
embroidery and the making of handsome costumes. All
the district that is now Morley was originally conceived
by the Indians to be a great giant, who named natural
features of the landscape after parts of his body; the
Knee Hills, the Hand Hills, Elbow River (that joins the
Bow at Calgary), and Ghost River.

Passing the station at Morley I see only certain small,

Banff Springs Hotel and Golf Course

neat buildings. All the homes of the Stonys are out of sight of the train. . . .

Along through the flat river bottom, far-away mountains, purplish in their shadows, and with snowy white crevasses in their peaks, show an increasing grandeur. . . . We are nearing the great upheaval of the earth's crust called the Rocky Mountains. Edward Whymper, famous mountaineer who climbed the Matterhorn, said the Rockies were equal to fifty Switzerlands. By the way, what a name for a brave man—Whymper (whimper)! Perhaps the man hated his name and in trying to overcome the effect of it became a hero. But, to get back to the Rockies: from Gap which we are approaching, they run 600 miles to Mission, near the Pacific Coast. Is there anywhere in the world, I wonder, a longer line of magnificent mountain scenery?

Far to the south the sky remains bright, while ahead grey clouds hang low about a scarred mountain whose erratic shoulders shut out the sun.

Seebe—We stop on a siding to let an eastbound train go through (railroad etiquette gives eastbound trains precedence over those bound west). . . . Our train goes on again, crossing a long iron bridge that spans a widening Bow River. . . .

Kananaskis—Name of a mythical Cree chief, meaning: "tall-straight-pine-with-branches-near-the-top." Kananaskis means to me Claude Brewster's famous dude ranch, which Dan and I expect to visit for some riding, and all because of those boots I found in the attic!

Exshaw—I catch sight of cement works. Two tracks here, and sidings. . . . Grotto mountain towers into the sky 8,880 feet. (Figure eights will probably pursue us all day! One good turn deserves another!) On single track again, and passing track-workers. . . .

Who-o-o-f! Roaring and reverberating sounds whirl around us from steep rock cliffs on each side; this is the Gap, a narrow way through . . . into the kingdom of the Rockies!

Bankhead—Cold comes down from the high mountains; altitude now of 4,581 feet. . . . Dan, who has been talking with a pleasant-looking man on the other side of the car, gets up and comes toward me as the train begins to slow down. Looking ahead over the open side of the car I feel a tingle of excitement as I see Banff station, its grounds ablaze with bright flowers, and, beyond it, mountains towering up into the sky.

BANFF

"Look," I said to Dan, who was all eyes as the hotel bus crossed Bow River Bridge and started up Spray Avenue, "this is a cute place," and I handed him a town-site plan I'd picked up somewhere. "The avenues are called after rivers, and all the streets in Banff are named for wild animals." As Dan was glancing at the plan, our

bus swung into a handsome courtyard and we saw before us towered and terraced Banff Springs Hotel.

In a galleried lobby, Mr. Deyell, the manager, made
us welcome, and after the usual preliminaries a porter
took us up to our apartment.

The room we entered had an eastern exposure that
was mostly glass. Passing straight to the windows as the
porter disposed of the luggage, Dan and I looked out.

Below, in a green terrace bordered with flowers, a
fountain played, while figures in bright colours moved
about or leaned on a stone balustrade looking down upon
a lower terrace in the midst of which was a bathing-
pool, its waters glinting in the noontide brightness.
There, a dozen men and women were swimming, or adding to their tan, chatting while they reclined on sun-
warmed turf. But it wasn't this we gazed at; it was the
scene, far below and beyond, of a valley that lay at the
base of towering Mount Rundle, on the east, where the
waters of Bow and Spray Rivers met; and of Tunnel Mountain on the west, wide, and open to the sun,
stretching on in green and watered loveliness to the distant snow-clad barrier of Fairholm Range, the Valley of
the Bow.

Most sea-level folk feel the altitude (4,700 feet) upon
arriving at Banff; Dan and I were no exceptions. We put
off long walks till the following day and spent our first
afternoon in becoming acquainted with the hotel, hav-

ing tea at Fairholme Lounge, and wandering through the grounds. In the evening we joined other guests in Mount Stephen Hall and listened to an informative lecture entertainingly given by Dan McCowan, a well-known Canadian naturalist.

The next morning we both felt adjusted to the altitude and took a walk up Sulphur Mountain to visit the Alpine Club, Mr. Calhoun of Calgary having introduced us. We were given a hearty welcome and invited to luncheon. It was jolly to meet mountain climbers whom we might see again in their August encampment in Little Yoho Valley.

Walking down to the village from the Alpine Club we stopped for awhile at the Cascades of Time, an enchanting place where one may watch water falling over rocks of every geological age, and sit in rustic seats beside pools set in the midst of Alpine shrubs and bright blossoming flowers.

Dan went off to play golf on the morning of our third day in Banff. Remembering I had promised to meet him at the Golf Club, about noon I walked across the turf that borders the swimming-pool, where bathers were disporting themselves, and took a path that led downward, under trees. Rustic seats invited me to pause and enjoy the forest, but this time I kept along to the viaduct spanning a stream. Crossing it, I came to the Club

House, set high above Spray River.

In a balcony overlooking the clear, shallow, rippling waters of Spray River, parties were seated at tables enjoying an outdoor luncheon. From where I sat I saw across the swiftly running waters of the Spray a fairway of emerald-green grass that ran along the base of

Mount Rundle, and far to the right blue-green peaks lifted themselves into a sky that hadn't a single cloud. But Dan didn't come.

I went down to the lower terrace of the Golf Club, where I talked with the caddie master. In answer to my various questions, he told me that the seventh hole, of this 18-hole, mile-high course, is carved out of the mountainside. Seeing it through the trees near the fairway, one is faced by the sheer rock wall of Mount Rundle, and this has given it the name of "Gibraltar." I learned that the first tee of the course, below the terrace where I stood, is 50 feet above Spray River, with a carry of 150 yards. What interested me more was to hear that the grasses for this course were determined on after long research, and that trainloads of top soil were necessary to build the course, which is surrounded by a 12-foot-high wire fence to protect it from elk, deer, and bears.

At this point Dan's foursome came in; he had enjoyed himself on the beautiful course and was ready for a good luncheon. While we ate we made a plan to leave the next day (July 11) for a trip to Emerald Lake, Yoho Valley, Lake O'Hara and Lake Louise, arranging it so that we should get back to Banff for the Indian Days that begin on July 26.

CHAPTER VII

MR. MOOSE OF EMERALD LAKE

At dusk on our second evening at Emerald Lake I went fishing, and in an hour brought back a string of trout that surprised the Duchess. I took the trout up to the Chalet, and an admiring chef agreed to have them cooked for our breakfast. It was after this, while talking with some of the guests, that I heard about a moose that lately had been seen in this vicinity.

"Do you mean," I asked, "that the moose has been seen near here?"

"Oh yes," my informant answered; "he seems to have headquarters to the left of the bridge where the forest meets a small arm of Emerald Lake." Our conversation then drifted on to other topics.

Early next morning, before breakfast (I enjoy the early hours), I started out for a walk, and had just reached the bridge when off to the left I suddenly saw a great antlered moose standing up to his belly in water and busily eating whatever it was he got by plunging his head under the surface of the lake. This was the first moose I had ever looked upon in his native habitat, and the sight gave me a thrill. Much excited, I rushed back up the hill to our bungalow to get my camera, hoping the creature would stay where he was. Five minutes later, when I was again at the bridge, the moose was standing in the same spot.

As I drew near, the Bull Moose looked toward me with a preoccupied expression and complete indifference, continuing to chew his corn flakes. Just as the shutter of my camera clicked, up came his big head, as though he had heard something; and floundering ashore he disappeared in a second among trees of the bordering forest.

"Great news, Duchess!" I called as I ran up the steps of the bungalow. "I've just shot a moose!"

"How terrible!" she exclaimed. "What in the world shall we do with the poor thing?"

"I'm going to have him developed," I explained laughing. "He's in the camera."

That same day, well mounted, and with Tabby, the picturesque guide of Emerald Lake, the Duchess and I took our first Rocky Mountain ride. We were glad to turn in early.

I was awakened about dawn the following day by an outlandish noise that seemed right under our windows. Jumping up I looked out. There, with four sharp hoofs and antlered head, and so close I could have put my hand on him, stood Mr. Moose!

Emerald Lake and Glacier

Now, it's a funny thing how the mind works. What I instantly thought of upon seeing this great creature were the flower beds up at the Chalet—those brilliant borders which, viewed against the unbelievable green of the lake and its distant background of dark forested mountain-sides, take one's breath away. Along with thought of the flowers there flashed an image of the young man from Vancouver Island who so lovingly had them in charge.

"Moose! Flowers!" I thought, and, not waiting to reason out what the animal's intentions might be, I jammed my feet into a pair of slippers, and, in striped pyjamas, rushed out of the bungalow. My burning thought was, "If I don't do something, the gardener's labour of weeks will go to make a Continental breakfast for a moose."

We met face to face in the road. The moose, seeing something he had never seen before jumping up and down in front of him, lowered his head and gave me a dirty look. Now, only a day or so earlier, when leafing through a publication of the Canadian Pacific Railway about big game hunting, I had come upon a photograph of a moose in this same position, and under it were printed the words, "When he turns, look out!"

I groaned inwardly. Oh, why had I neglected my opportunities to learn how to converse with a moose? Suddenly this one wagged his short tail, his tongue came out, and I swear he seemed to lick his chops. A terrible thought flashed: Was he carnivorous?

I jumped into the air waving striped arms and legs. The creature stood his ground. I went into a whirling Dervish act. The moose was plainly puzzled. Suddenly he turned and started for the Chalet. I was right after him. It wasn't "Curfew shall not ring tonight" that I was saying to myself, but "Moose shall not eat flowers for breakfast." I was mad now, clear through, and, as I loped up the hill at the moose's heels, I made up my mind to grab him by the tail. That, I thought, would make him change his direction. The moose must have been psychic, able to read my mind, because now he suddenly side-stepped to take a look at me. Plainly my stripes were too much to be borne. Mr. Moose leaped across the road in front of me, kept on down the steep bank, and plunged into Emerald Lake.

When I got back to our bungalow I tried to be quiet, and in being so fell over a chair.

"What on earth is the matter?" cried the Duchess, sitting up. "Why are you wandering around before sunrise in those terrible pyjamas? How in the world an artist with a sense of colour could possibly buy such things is more than I—"

"Go back to sleep, Duchess," I murmured; "all is lovely. I've just kept tryst with a moose."

The Duchess's Diary

July 9, 8:30 P. M.:—The evening air, aromatic with fragrance of balsam, is stirring blossoms of the flower boxes near me as I sit on the porch of Maid-o'-the-Mountain bungalow gazing upon Emerald Lake, and across its waters to a steep spruce-covered shore that rises, darkly now, to meet at mountain top the evening sky.

Dan is out on the lake in a canoe, floating on a surface of liquid emeralds, trying to catch fish. Why spoil so perfect an hour?

My spirits are soaring to meet the mountain peaks that guard from almost every wind this silent and beautiful spot. Our bungalow, part way down a steep hill from Chalet and Club House, gives a sense of retirement that is refreshing, as well as a superb view from this end of the lake to the other. I am happy, sitting here, as it were on my own porch, yet removed from all the obligations in which my own porch would involve me.

After the thrills that played octaves up and down my emotional spine this afternoon, while the Canadian Pacific train made its astonishing way from Banff to Field, this place, like a pause in music, this friendly aloofness brings wholeness to the spirit at the day's end.

A newspaper I picked up for a moment at the Chalet

after dinner (an excellent dinner, by the way) told of intense heat in the States and parts of Canada; this is difficult to realize as I sit here wearing a coat.

July 12:—In the lobby of Emerald Lake Chalet at luncheon time today, whom should we come upon but Dr. John May of Cohasset, Mass., who helped to salvage our tent one wild night on the Gaspé Peninsula. It was pleasant to exchange with him news of three years' wanderings. And, too, we met Mrs. Deyell, the charming young wife of the manager of Banff Springs Hotel; she drove over from Banff with her sister. Mr. and Mrs. Hulbert-Powell—an engaging couple from Cambridge (Trinity College), England—after luncheon came to bid us good-bye. They have been making a visit here that she might paint the native wild flowers.

The sequestered peace of Emerald Lake was momentarily broken, early this afternoon, by the arrival of three long grey and blue buses that swept up to the Chalet out of a world that all of us on the porch had left behind days ago. A ripple of excitement ran through the crowd, reminding me of that which always stirs the spectators when a steamer comes into port. As I gazed upon these mechanized coaches of a modern world, silhouetted against the emerald waters and the deeply wooded mountainsides of our retreat, they seemed to change, to turn mysteriously into so many pumpkin coaches newly arrived from fairyland. And even as I watched, they rolled away. . . .

Veils of mist from the noontide shower dissolved, revealing newly washed clouds hung up to dry around the craggy tops of Mount Carnarvon, Emerald Peak, and Mount Burgess. Soon the sun came forth, shining gloriously upon a fresh, green world.

Dan and I started out for a walk to Lone Duck Lake by way of a narrow trail, soft under foot with humus of many a fallen leaf. Woodland flowers starred the golden gloom beneath tall trees. All along we saw twin-flowers and anemones, the white beauty of bunchberry blossoms recurring like the loved refrain of a familiar song.

About us the silent air, filled with pungent fragrance of balsam, and the gleam of moist leaves, delicately stirring, brought wholeness to the heart. An objective one must have, even when merely taking a walk; but what happens on the way to it is what constitutes life. Dan and I never reached Lone Duck Lake, but that does not matter; nor do we lose these enchanting woodland aisles because tomorrow we must leave them behind; their beauty has become part of ourselves and so it is ours for always.

EMERALD LAKE TO YOHO VALLEY LODGE

July 13, 9:15 A. M.:—The slender, fair young man who drove Dan and me four days ago from Field station up through the balsam woods of Snow Peak Avenue to this lake we are now leaving is again our driver, and again I am seated beside him that I may hear clearly all he will tell us along the way to Yoho Valley Lodge.

Mrs. Jackson, the hostess, with others on the porch of Emerald Lake Chalet, stands waving us good-bye as this motor coach glides away, down the hill and over the bridge spanning Emerald Creek. I give a quick glance right, to the house and corral of Tabby the guide, who took me on my first Rocky Mountain ride; then the car swings left and we are on the highway with jack pine, lodgepole pine, and spruce close beside us on either hand. . . .

When within sight of Mount Stephen, we see far up toward its towering peak the entrance to Monarch Silver Mines, looking from here like a mouse hole. The miners are carried up and down the mountain in "buckets" operated by cables. I wonder what the effect is on the men of burrowing into the earth at a high altitude?

Half an hour's ride from Emerald Lake we pass into the Government area of Yoho National Park. Now, the wild white anger of Kicking Horse River is beside us as our car runs along a ledge—is swung by the driver to the outside of a curve! and stopped, that we all may gaze from an elevation of 4,168 feet upon the meeting of two mighty rivers—Yoho, yellow and dirty from the melting of Daly Glacier, coming steeply down to plunge at right angles into the crystal clear waters of the Kick-

ing Horse! A grand sight. . . . We drive on through
breath-taking scenery. . . . About ten o'clock we start
to ascend Mount Field. An ingenious switch-back and
excellent driving combined to get us up 200 feet in a
third of a mile. I sat looking on, thrilled at the nice
young man's performance, and devoutly hoping that we
would not have to leave the middle of the way to let a
car pass. . . . Hurrah! We are safely up to the height
we were aiming at, and—here comes the car I felt was
in the offing—a moment too late, thank Heaven, for
drama.

Up here on the top there is a glorious view. Mount
Wapta and many peaks are visible, while back of us
Cathedral Mountain lifts its 10,000 (odd) feet into the
sky.

The coach rolls along . . . then another stop is made
that we may look down far below into the steep rocky
canyon of the Yoho; its waters come boiling and plunging toward us. . . . After a pause we proceed and in a
few minutes the end of the route is reached at the foot
of magnificent Takakkaw Falls. Before I get out to join
the other passengers in walking nearer to the spectacle,
the driver tells me that the Indian word *Takakaw*,
means "fed-by-the-sun." A tremendous volume of
water from melting Daly Glacier pouring over a precipice above where we are standing plunges in clouds of
foam down the sheer face of rock to this level 1,200

feet below. A quick-flowing river formed by the falls runs away to the south. Only the Falls of Yosemite in California, 1,280 feet, and the Falls of Victoria Nyanza in South Africa, highest in the world, exceed these Falls of Takakkaw.

Dan has been in ecstacies all the way from Emerald; now, after the wonders he and I have looked upon this morning, we get back into the coach, speechless, and in five minutes find ourselves at Yoho Valley Lodge.

Mount Burgess, Emerald Lake

CHAPTER VIII

YOHO VALLEY

The Duchess's Diary

July 14, 10 P. M.:—This morning the living-room of
Yoho Valley Lodge was warm with orange and golden
colour and the leaping flames of a log fire, when Mrs.
McAndless, the attractive hostess of the Lodge, intro-
duced to us Mr. and Mrs. William T. Kelley of Chicago
and two young men from Zeeland, Michigan—Mr.
Walter van Haitsma and his assistant and friend Mr.
Jerry Van de Vusse. (The nice Dutch names! Whenever
Holland is mentioned I think of my friend the distin-
guished scholar of Columbia University, New York,
Adrian J. Barnouw, who has translated the *Canterbury
Tales* into his native Dutch language.) But to get back
to this morning—the living-room instantly became, to
me, a background for the dark beauty of Mrs. Kelley.
Clothed in russet and touched with the gleam of gold,
she made me hope the rain would continue all day that
I might sit in that glowing room and look at her.

Six travellers, a piano and an open fire ought to produce something. In this case four of us told stories; Mr. van Haitsma showed superb photographs he had taken of the Rocky Mountains and played accompaniments for songs Mr. Van de Vusse sang. Out of this entertainment came a plan to ride next day, if fair, to Twin Falls Tea House. Knowing nothing about the trail I agreed to go, quite as though I were an old hand, but my eye roved the room for a cushion I might appropriate—a small cushion to put on my saddle before mounting—and I spotted one on a sofa. My ride at Emerald Lake four days ago made a deep impression on me—too deep. I am bearing the mark of it still!

"If we start before noon tomorrow," said Mrs. Kelley, who knows and adores this country, "we will reach Twin Falls by three o'clock, and after tea there will be time to climb to Yoho Glacier."

("Woman," I said to myself, "what are you getting into? Your will power is in good working order, and your boots—*the* boots—have been expertly shod with bright Hungarian hobnails by Banff's most skilful boot surgeon; but what about your experience?" From within came the answer: "Even the job of living has to be taken on without experience in order to get the experience which alone enables one to live. Go to it.") So, as we all walked toward the dining-room for luncheon, I remarked casually, "See you tomorrow."

And not least among the pleasures of this rainy day at Yoho Valley Lodge have been the delicious meals.

Twin Falls Tea House, July 15, 4:45 P. M.:—From the depths of a comfortable chair in the Tea House living-room, warmed by a big wood-burning stove and comforted by a recent hot dinner, "I take up my pencil" to record the events of this day. Not that I can ever forget the incidents of my second Rocky Mountain ride, but from this point of achievement it will be a pleasure to write of them in the past tense. (That word "tense" creeps in here I see, as in fact it has been with me all day.) "Notes of a tenderfoot" would be a suitable title for what I am about to write now in the interval before the crowd returns from an excursion to Yoho Glacier. It is unbelievable that, on top of the trip up here, everybody should want to go right out after having got warm, and ride part way down the mountain again in order to walk up a windy canyon and gaze upon ice, acres of it—but that is what the Kelleys, Dan and the others have just left here to do. They can have it all with my blessing. I am a happy woman to be right where I am.

This morning at eleven o'clock (it seems a month ago) six of us met at the corral of Yoho Lodge, as planned. Harold the guide mounted us—Mrs. Kelley on handsome Gloria; her husband on a roan called Prince; two young women from Syracuse, New York, Miss Bowers, Miss Van Brughler, on good-looking beasts; Dan on big Tabasco; and I, with Mrs. McAndless's pillow under me, on little bay Brownie. (Van and Jerry had gone on early to photograph.) Riding his own beautiful slender black horse, Harold led the way out to the highway, then left, along past the thundering waters of Takakkaw Falls and north till we reached a trail to the left. Here we made a detour of a few minutes for sight of water falling in a delicate pattern over a rock face—Point Lace Falls. Back on the main way, we went on a short distance and then made a second detour to the right, and soon came to a splendid fall of water called Angel Stairs. We wheeled our seven horses in a narrow space between crowding trees and returned over the rough track to the main way. Twenty hours of rain had made earth and rocks slippery, which we all found out when a few minutes later Harold led us into the narrow forest trail to Twin Falls.

Forty minutes passed and I was still on Brownie's back, both legs intact, in spite of the nearness of tree trunks each side of the way. I began to feel confidence stealing over me. "This isn't so bad," I thought. And then we came to Yoho River! It was not raging at this point, but it was a lot of water running swiftly.

Yobo Glacier

"Do I have to go through that?" I asked myself, and the answer was yes. All the other horses, hesitating while picking a place to cross, finally plunged in, and Brownie with the others. The water didn't come quite up to my boots, and when Brownie made the other bank and we were again going along on dry land I felt well on the way to being a horsewoman.

Rain held off though skies above us were grey. About half past one the trail became (to me) hair-raising. Our horses, in a line, one after the other, plodded or scrambled up and up, save for momentary pauses. There was much of beauty around us, but I was intent on making good, on this first long ride, and I kept my eyes mostly on where Brownie was putting her feet.

When, a little after three o'clock, we reached the corral of Twin Falls, and dismounted, it was a happy landing for me. Now that I'm here safely and know the way, I'd like to do it all over again tomorrow and see what everything on the trail up really looks like.

❦

After a bountiful hot meal at Twin Falls Tea House, about half past three o'clock, the nine of us who had ridden up from Yoho Valley Lodge rose from the table and settled ourselves comfortably around the big wood-burning stove. Cigarettes and a pipe or two were tinging the air with a pleasant aroma when someone asked, "What about going to Yoho Glacier?"

The Duchess, who had stretched out her boots to the heat and was just beginning to purr, looked quickly around the circle.

"Ice!" she exclaimed. "Is it possible anyone wants to go look at ice?"

Miss Bowers from northern New York laughed and, much amused, replied:

"We really ought to see the Yoho Glacier. It covers twenty square miles of earth, and it isn't far from here—the remains, you know, of the last Ice Age."

"The remains will lie in peace as far as I am concerned," said the Duchess with a twinkle in her eye. "This country has pulled my mind all crooked as it is, by the strain it puts on the imagination. Here we are talking about ice that capped the climax for life æons ago, and a few miles away men are digging out of Mount Stephen fossils of creatures that sported around Yoho Valley when it was nothing but ocean." Through the pipe smoke and laughter the Duchess added a last word as she settled back in her chair:

"All of you be prehistoric if you will. I shall stay right here till I'm thoroughly toasted, then I shall go out and make the acquaintance of Twin Falls. In the meanwhile there will be an opportunity to ponder on the peculiarities of man."

Harold had guessed that most of us would want to see the glacier and had left the horses saddled. When we all got to the corral I offered Tabasco a handful of sugar, feeling a bit sorry to take him down the mountain again. To my astonishment he merely smelled of it, then turned his head away.

"Offer him some of that," said Harold, indicating a pile of hay that had been brought up from Yoho Lodge (as every least thing has to be brought), and Tabasco mouthed the handful I gave him as though hay were the most delicious food in the world. It's all in the point of view!

As soon as we were mounted, Harold led off down the steep part of the trail that we had come up less than two hours before. Near the bottom we turned to the left and at once began to climb, up and up, till the trees thinned, and in a few minutes we came out upon a bare, open space.

Before us, across a stony valley threaded by a stream, rose a mountain as barren as the one immediately on our left; and far off to the left, between these two, showing silverly against the dark sky, gleamed the great ice wedge of Yoho Glacier.

Never have I looked upon a scene so expressive of desolation. There, ice and all the winds of heaven held sway. And how the wind sucked down through that stony valley which once had been filled with ice—for this is an inactive glacier that is receding instead of moving forward. But whether going or coming, Yoho Glacier suggests to the imagination a frozen nightmare.

After looking at this scene a moment we dismounted, tethered our horses to some bushes and prepared to get to the ice level. This meant making our way downhill amongst boulders and rubble—hard going for perhaps half a mile. The air grew continually colder as we drew nearer the ice, while the wind, blowing down upon us from the great ice sheet that, far away, cut a line of white against the threatening sky, felt as though it had been chilled since the beginning of time.

After much scrambling we finally reached the foot of the glacier—actually stood upon it. The appearance of the ice was weird, coloured with deposit from soil erosion; it suggested millions of tons of molasses candy that had suddenly congealed.

Underneath the glacial ice we heard the sound of water, and in places saw water rushing into caverns, and knew that it finally emerged as the narrow stream we saw running down the valley—Yoho River. The colour of the ice in these caverns was clear and blue, unbelievably beautiful, not like the upper ice covered with the rubble and dirt from erosion of surrounding mountains.

Mrs. Kelley has a strange passion for glaciers. While

Tea House, Twin Falls, Yobo Valley, B.C.

she and Mr. Kelley were making photographic records of the ice formations, I was trying to put my impressions on paper, without much success. If I should try to draw from memory what I saw, it would look like a nightmare.

The guide warned us not to venture far upon the ice, and all of us knew it was no place for those without experience. As for me, I was perfectly willing to leave the ice to the Ice Age and call it a day; and when Harold suggested we all start to return to Twin Falls, there wasn't a moment's hesitation on the part of any of us.

In climbing again to the higher level, Harold pointed out to us the great peaks, far away, of LeFroy and Victoria mountains, that rise above Lake Louise. The horses were glad to see us. I'm sure they had been saying among themselves, "Why in time do these people want to come to a crazy place like this?"

Once mounted, we went downhill much faster than we had come; and when we turned up the last steep stretch, the horses went at the trail as though their minds were filled with thoughts of hay and of the corral where they would have nothing to do but eat.

It was after six thirty when they brought us up onto the last level. Leaving the horses to Harold's good care, we all hurried past the grand spectacle of Twin Falls whose thunder filled the evening air, and what a welcome sight the log house was, with smoke pouring from its chimney!

The Duchess was waiting for us, when we barged into the living-room, and, as we pulled off coats and extra sweaters, said in reply to our questions, "Oh, I've had a lovely afternoon, meeting the Twin Falls porcupine."

I didn't know how hungry one could get, up in these mountains, but Mrs. McAndless knew. She and Mrs. Florance rode the long trail from Yoho Valley Lodge alone to bring up extra supplies of food. They arrived about seven o'clock and an hour afterward, with darkness gathering, cheerfully leaped on their horses and with a laugh dashed away down the trail to the valley. Riding from Yoho Lodge to Twin Falls, a big adventure to us, is but an incident in the day, to those who know this country.

Soon after dinner we were all tucked in our beds upstairs, under plenty of good wool blankets. The next thing we knew it was morning; smell of wood smoke, coffee, and frying bacon awakened us to fresh adventures.

CHAPTER IX

HIGHLINE TRAIL

"What is the trail going to be like today?" asked the Duchess of the crowd busily engaged in tucking away a good breakfast.

"The Highline Trail to Yoho Valley is one of the most rewarding in the Canadian Rockies," answered Mr. Kelley, a resident of Chicago who cherishes deep enthusiasm for the world's high places. "As we follow it today we shall have views of five great glaciers, as well as waterfalls, peaks, and mountain ranges; and part of the time, way below us, the magnificent Yoho River Valley."

"Below us, did you say?" asked the Duchess raising her eyebrows. "I haven't forgotten the shelf seven thousand feet above Yoho River that we rode along yesterday with nothing but a precipice to comfort me. Are you suggesting that today we shall ride around the eyelids of mountains thousands of feet up in the air? If so I'll have another cup of coffee!"

"Watch your metaphors, Duchess," I called from the foot of the table. "If they get into your scrambled eggs

[79]

we shan't be able to save you!" Amid good-natured laughter we finished breakfast.

Out of doors, thunder of the Falls filled the air. Lifting our gaze high up to the top of the Barrier Rim that faced us, we took a last look at the two torrential streams (from Glacier des Poilus) rushing over its edge to fall headlong down the sheer face, and with terrific impact break upon boulders 600 feet below. The resulting clouds of spray and mist rising into the air almost reached us where we stood, fascinated by the magnificent spectacle.

The voice of Miss Bowers calling "The horses are ready," brought us back to the day's business. Taking leave of the kind hostess who had made our visit overnight so comfortable, Miss "Burgh," the Duchess, the Kelleys, Van, Jerry and I hurried along to the corral where Harold was cheerfully awaiting us.

A package of lunch was tied to each saddle, and a raincoat that each rider was hoping he would not have to put on. The good horses turned to look at us with detached expressions as we gave them friendly pats. We mounted and one after the other our horses fell into line, Harold's leading, and took the steep forest trail to the left that gave us glimpses now and then, as we went up, of the Tea House, growing smaller and smaller to sight.

About half past nine we came out into the open, at

the end of a bridge which spanned a swiftly flowing stream. This was the place where we were to give up the horses and hike; so, after we dismounted, Harold, riding his handsome black, got all the loose horses before him, then, with a wave of his hat and a "See you later," drove them back down the trail out of our sight. We would meet him again about noon.

After crossing the bridge we all stopped to look at the amazing view. I think everyone felt very much alone in the midst of immensities. No guide, no horse, no special knowledge of the trail we were to follow.

Toward the south we looked down into Yoho Valley, and above it saw Mount Niles and the great Daly Glacier. To the east the Lilliput Ice Field was gleaming and at our backs the Glacier des Poilus and Whaleback Mountain. What were eight little humans among such giants?

Eyes filled with the magnificent panorama, we moved along. The trail led gently upward. There were no trees, only scrub growth and many alpine flowers. The altitude was beginning to shorten my breathing; some of the others felt it too. Four of the crowd were stopping frequently to take photographs. The Duchess, going along by herself way ahead of me, was apparently gathering blossoms of certain alpine plants that grow on these uplands.

We paid no attention to time, each one sitting to rest

and take in the unbelievably beautiful views when he or she felt like it, or catching up with the others, as it happened to suit the fancy.

The trail narrowed till it was not more than a foot wide. Time went on, and we reached a place where the trail was cut into the side of a shale mountain, with nothing to speak of below us as far as the eye could see. The Duchess, right behind me, suddenly remarked that she thought she would close her eyes and hang on to my coat tail, but I reached a hand back that she clung to until the barren terrifying stretch ended in an arm's length of green growth on each side of us.

The descending trail led to a series of switch-backs down the mountainside. Ahead of us the two young women from Syracuse, gaily ignoring this slower means of getting down, cut across the switch-backs in a straight run to the bottom. The Duchess and I zigzagged steeply down through increasingly luxurious growth of bushes and trees to the bank of Little Yoho River, and there found the girls sitting on a bit of rail fence talking to Harold, who had all the horses heading up the river waiting to go.

When the rest of the party had got to the bottom, each one mounted and, single file, keeping beside the river, rode beneath forest trees, up Little Yoho Valley.

There were vistas ahead that I wish I could have sketched, as we went along to higher levels. At about one-thirty we rode into a beautiful glade beside Little Yoho River and found ourselves in the 1937 encampment of the famous Alpine Club.

Although the official opening of the camp was three days off, we were given a hearty welcome by Colonel Tweedy, the Secretary of the Alpine Club whom we had enjoyed meeting in Banff; and he very kindly invited us to take shelter in a big tent from the light rain which had begun to fall. There we ate the lunches we had brought along and were greatly fortified by hot coffee, which the Colonel provided us. Afterward, the rain having stopped, we all went out to take a look at the camp.

The number enrolled for the 1937 annual encampment of the Alpine Club was so large that tents to accommodate the crowd gleamed whitely beneath the spruce and pine trees of a wide area beside Little Yoho River. We were told that in the next few days about a hundred climbers would be here for their annual attack on the surrounding mountains and glaciers, adding that one party was to camp right on the Yoho Glacier! My experience at Yoho Glacier the day before made me wish those hardy ones luck.

In the big conference tent the Colonel pointed out to me the bulletin board upon which day by day a schedule of climbs is posted.

"We are very careful about our climbers," said the

Colonel. "Each one is required to write down his or her name and the climb he or she wishes to make; then a committee looks up each one's record and, if anyone is not considered qualified to take the climb he desires, he is told to choose a less difficult one."

The huge cook tent of the camp was a marvel of efficient arrangement, considering the surrounding wilderness, and my mouth watered as I saw three cooks preparing a meal for those already in camp.

The Colonel showed us his own tent, because the Duchess was eager to know just how a real balsam bough bed was constructed. When she saw the fragrant branches neatly interlaced and piled one upon another till they rose a foot or more above the ground, forming the most delightful inner-spring mattress imaginable, she sighed and said:

"Why didn't our parents start us mountain climbing as soon as we were out of our cradles? If they had," turning to the Colonel, "we should now be able to accept the invitation your Club so kindly has given us to spend a week here in camp with your members."

With a laugh the three of us returned to where the others were gathered. While we were mounting, a pack of twenty horses driven by two men, came into the clearing. It didn't seem five minutes before those men had their horses tethered to bushes all over the place, and were unroping the packs and stripping them from

the patient beasts. It takes a tremendous stock of supplies to provide for the wants of a hundred people in
the wilderness, and every bit of it must be brought in
on the backs of horses.

It was a little more than half past two when our
party bade the Alpiners good-bye and, following Harold,
rode along the river to a fording place. When his black
horse plunged into the swiftly flowing stream, one
after the other our horses followed. The Duchess, who
was singing: "One More River to Cross," had to prod
Brownie with her heels to get him into the water. Out
again on the other bank of Little Yoho River, Harold
swerved up to the right, away from the homeward
trail, and rode his horse up through the rough and
between trees, with the rest of us blindly following.
Suddenly we came out on the very edge of the President
Glacier. Mrs. Kelley, strangely moved by sight of ice
thousands of years old, said, "I long to put my hand
upon it!" Ice and emotion, hand in hand, seemed strange
to me; yet I myself felt thrilled to be looking at frozen
water that had been imprisoned here since the Ice Age.
Five minutes later, wheeling our horses, we made a
breakneck descent to the main trail, heading south.

Now our way was through alpine meadows and
steadily ascended—the President Range on our right;
far below, on our left, the glorious Yoho Valley, glorious
even though grey was tempering the colours of the scene.

Our horses, following the Highline Trail, brought us to Lookout Point, a breath-taking place up 7,000 feet, that seems to hang in space between the far distant valley and the wide, overarching heavens. We reined in our horses and gazed about at the cyclorama of wonders. To south and west were range after range of snow-capped peaks and gleaming glaciers. Neither the Duchess nor I can ever forget that scene.

Starting along from Lookout Point, we saw winding below us the ledges we were to follow.

At an altitude of 7,000 feet, our horses, head to tail, began pacing along narrow ledges that wound around cliff after cliff bare of trees. Tabasco and I kept to the end of the line; I liked to have in front of me the changing pictures made by the riders. Sometimes looping of the trail brought a right angle turn that gave less space than a horse really needed and, after getting his head and shoulders pointing one way, he had a hard time to find room on the ledge for his hind hoofs, but he always won through.

Watching the marvellous beauty of the scene all about me, I became lost in thought. We were in a particularly barren stretch of mountainside, without a bush or twig to break the steep drop to a bottom far below, when I was suddenly brought back to reality by Kelley's horse just in front of Tabasco. He was prodding with his head the horse in front of him, which happened to be

Gloria. As I watched, Gloria registered her objection to this badinage by a swing of her hind quarters, and her hind hoofs broke over the edge of the 12-inch ledge. For a fraction of a second anything might have happened—it was due to the Kelleys' cool-headedness that nothing did—during which there flashed before me a picture of the whole bunch of horses, with this for a cue, reverting to the ways of their wild ancestors and starting a cross country race for the bottom. It was just as well that the Duchess was up in front next to Harold and did not see this bit of side play; it might have had a depressing effect upon her.

The ledges brought us slowly down to rough footing on glacial debris at the base of cliffs. Riding through a shallow, swiftly flowing stream, we took to a trail that now wound gently along mountain slopes and beside the welcome green of pine trees, bringing us, toward four-thirty, to a place near Summit Lake, where three trails meet.

Harold stopped us all to ask if we wanted to ride over Yoho Pass and take a look at Emerald Lake before going home. Everyone preferred to continue right on to Yoho Valley, so the patient horses moved forward, keeping to the trail on the left.

From my place at the end of the line I watched the riders strung out ahead of me. There was nothing above us now but the sky; we were on top of the rim that seemed so high and far away when two days ago we had looked up at it from Yoho Valley Lodge.

To our left and further down than we could see, Yoho River, I knew, was running. Had the sun been shining we could have seen, directly across the valley, the white fall of Takakkaw's waters.

Way ahead of me, Harold, toward whom I happened to be looking, suddenly disappeared as completely as though he had ridden over the edge of the world. While I was wondering what had swallowed him up, the Duchess, just behind Harold, vanished in the same way. I rubbed my eyes, but all that did was to let me see each one of our party wiped out in the same manner. It was laughable, and I hurried Tabasco to learn the reason.

When I myself got to the place where all this happened, I found I was on the edge of the rim, and saw that the trail from there plunged precipitately down the mountain in zigzagging switch-backs. I was just in time to catch a glimpse of the last rider disappearing between the trees far below.

Without a word from me, Tabasco stepped boldly down into a trough of mud that had been churned by the feet of eight horses, and bracing his legs he slid head first most of the way to the first right angle turn below. A few steps at that point and then Tabasco repeated the performance.

"What is this anyway," I asked myself, "a circus?"

But there wasn't time for imaginary conversation.

After turning the ninth point in the equine Shoot the Chutes, I saw in the trail below me a rock jutting out, and beside the rock a pine tree. Tabasco slid to the rock, and—I am happy to say—stopped. While he was turning himself for the next lap I looked over the rock and saw, nothing, unless you count blue haze.

"What is the Duchess doing about all this?" I thought as Tabasco and I continued our amazing progress head first toward the Valley. I had kept count and we were doing the twenty-eighth right angle turn when I realized that the trees had become much bigger and that there was lush green growth close about my course.

"Stick to it, Tabasco, old boy," I murmured to the good creature as we rounded the fifty-first switch-back; "there can't be much more of this." And there wasn't. At the fifty-second turn I saw through green branches the outbuildings at the back of Yoho Lodge; and then Tabasco and I shot out into the open. We had done the Highline Trail!

Harold was standing by, smiling and unconcerned as though switch-backs were nothing in his life. The Duchess, with the now famous pillow under one arm, turned in her course toward the Lodge and called back: "The Trail to Mount Assiniboine will surely seem a parlour game after this."

"Well anyway," answered Harold, "you're a little

better prepared for five days of rough riding. This Highline Trail is about as stiff a ride as any you'll be taking."

I got to the Lodge just as the Duchess, handing the pillow to smiling Mrs. McAndless, was saying, "But for these few feathers I should have been marooned among the glaciers for the rest of my life."

Breaking in I exclaimed, "May all the glaciers melt and run into the Pacific Ocean if they want to; what I want is *tea!*"

"And you're having it," laughed the Lady of the Lodge, "right now, in front of the living-room fire."

CHAPTER X

DAN GOES TO LAKE O'HARA

The Duchess's Diary

Friday, July 16, 2:30 P. M.:—This is the quiet time of day at Yoho Lodge. Most of the guests are off climbing or hiking or trail riding; among them Miss Georgia Englehardt, the famous Alpine climber, who arrived yesterday. She is slim and youthful and wears her fair hair cropped like a boy.

I am sitting in a canvas chair placed on the grass in front of our bungalow. Straight before me across the valley, and carrying my gaze up to the sky out of which it seems to pour, is the white water of Takakkaw Falls. I let my gaze circle from south of the Falls to north of them, and see that spired spruce form a horizontal band of green along the base of mountains whose rocky peaks cut a sky that today is serene blue. As my gaze ranges northward, noting the forestation of mountain flank or crest, I see the shadow of a cloud upon a green upland, and snow glittering upon an adjoining peak. In a deep curve between this peak and a sunny one to the west

[91]

shines the immemorial ice of Yoho Glacier.

Try as I will to look elsewhere, my gaze is inevitably brought back to the torrential waters of Takakkaw, ceaselessly falling in white majesty from high heaven down to a climactic loveliness of doom.

On the green slope below me, a fawn-coloured horse is grazing; he is Mrs. McAndless's Arabian, Spooks. For a long time this morning Spooks whinnied and whinnied for his friend Brownie, but Brownie did not come. Now, busily cropping the good green grass, Spooks is silent. Life must go on though the heart break. Even a horse grows philosophical.

Sunday night, July 18:—Dan went off to Lake O'Hara yesterday for several days of sketching and fishing. I preferred to stay here at Yoho. This morning Mr. van Haitsma, Van for short, and Jerry took me along on a photographing expedition. We left Yoho after breakfast, driving over the highway to Field. While we were parked for a moment near the railway station, along came Engine 2816 which brought Dan and me from Calgary. I waved to the engineer, and he gave me a snappy salute. Before leaving Field, Jerry drove to a gas station to have tires examined. The heat was terrific, so I got out of the car (an open one) and went into the clean and neat Brewster Garage. Looking around I saw on a wall a big sheet bordered with black, and bearing the title: Death Notice.

"Mercy!" I thought to myself, "has this place got anything to do with funerals?" Then I read the printed matter and found it was a warning about monoxide gas and the danger of having doors closed when an engine is running. Taking another look around the garage I saw, placed on top of a bag of oats, a nice accordion; and I thought, "all ready for the Dance of Death."

"Come, come," I said to myself, "stop juggling ideas." But just the same, if the stream of consciousness had been ice-cold water, I'd have tried to drink it, the heat made me so thirsty. At that moment Jerry called "All ready," and I dashed out into the hot sunshine. "Hold hard, Duchess," I said to myself, "this is a land of contrasts," and in five minutes we were speeding along a cool, shaded highway bound for Natural Bridge.

Evening. Jim, one of the guides here at Yoho, came along a few minutes ago leading Brownie, and, after un-hobbling Spooks, brought both horses up to me, stopping for a moment's chat. Jim said he was going to ride Brownie, and, after packing supplies on Spooks, drive him up to Twin Falls Tea House. That trip is fresh in my mind, and I should call it a day's job to ride up to Twin Falls and back. Jim spoke of the trip as an incident of a few hours. Well, it's all in the point of view!

Lake O'Hara Lodge
Hector, B.C.
Saturday, July 17.
2:30 P. M.

Oh, Duchess: I'm sending this back to you by "pony express" because my wild exit from Yoho Lodge early this morning may have got that imagination of yours to working overtime; here are a few facts to calm it down:

The 13-mile drive from Yoho Lodge to Lake Wapta Lodge took only about half an hour. As soon as we arrived, Van parked his car and he and Jerry set out on a photographing hike to Lake O'Hara. I'd like to have gone with them but had too much duffle so I applied at the Lodge office and got me a horse—name of Baldy, with white eyes. (Wapta Lodge is attractive, by the way; I want to fish in Wapta Lake before we go on to the Coast.) Baldy hated to leave his companions in the corral, but by the time I had got him across the railway tracks he decided to give up bucking his fate and plodded steadily along the eight-mile trail to Lake O'Hara.

The first four miles meant a steady climb for Baldy, through an open country of beautiful views. Lake O'Hara, you know, is 1,600 feet higher than Yoho Valley. Several times I caught sight of Van and Jerry away off on another trail where the going seemed to be hard. (They came into the Lodge a few minutes ago—two P. M., to have lunch—and said it had been heavy hiking but that they had got what they were after: good "shots.") Now, to go back:

Baldy and I were about half way to our destination

[94]

when two men, looking hot and bothered, stopped me to ask how much further they had to walk to reach Lake Wapta. Then a pack train passed me, going north, and looking at the bags on those horses started me thinking about what was in my own duffle bag. Had I brought my flies? I went over everything, mentally, and became convinced that I had forgotten to put them in. And here I was on the way to O'Hara for fishing! I could see you finding those flies somewhere in the bungalow at Yoho and having a fit because I would not be able to fish after all the planning to get to O'Hara. (Hold on, Duchess, till you get to the last page of this letter and you will feel better!)

All this about "flies" didn't add to my happiness, but I hoped something would turn up (you know my luck) to make everything come out right. And now my thoughts were momentarily diverted by what I saw approaching me—a guide, two pack horses and two other horses ridden by what looked like a father and daughter. When we all came up with one another "Father" called out:

"I'm having an awful time with my horse (the horse looked peaceful to me); I let him drink too much and now he has the colic. Don't let your horse drink much." Nodding an acknowledgment, I kept on going, wondering whether "Father" would finally have to walk home, when I saw down the trail coming toward me a woman in riding clothes. Instantly I felt she must be "Mother" and stopped Baldy. Before I could ask anything, she spoke, wiping her forehead—the sun was very hot.

"My horse tried to lie down on me, right on the trail. I'm too scared of him to ride any more, so I'm walking

[95]

back to Lake Wapta." It was hard not to laugh but I kept my face straight and tried to persuade her to take Baldy (he would have loved getting his head turned toward home) and ride the rest of the way; but she was finished with horses and refused to let me play the part of a Knight aiding a Lady in distress; so, I was forced to abandon her to her fate.

The second half of the ride was through forest, a beautiful shady trail; you would have loved it.

The first sight of Lake O'Hara, between tree trunks as the trail approaches its shore, is so beautiful it made me catch my breath and pull Baldy to a stop. I knew then why artists are so keen about this lake.

Baldy and I were following the trail along the edge of the Lake, and had come within sight of the Lodge, when suddenly a thunderous noise broke upon the serene stillness of noontide. I saw my old horse prick up his ears and took a double hold on the reins. The noise continued, increasing till it sounded like a hundred freight cars in a head-on railway collision. Astounded, and eager to know the why of it all, I rode quickly out of the forest and up to the group of people who were standing about in front of the Lodge. Everyone was looking up toward the south. In a moment I learned that I had just missed seeing a tremendous rock slide in the mountains about two miles away. So, Duchess, my entrance upon the scene at Lake O'Hara was not only dramatic; the orchestra was playing Wagnerian music.

And now comes comedy. As I signed the register, the pleasant hostess of Lake O'Hara Lodge saw my name. "There is a package waiting for you," she said and handed me what I found in a second were the flies and leaders that Mitcheltree the famous guide had promised to send me when I met him at Banff Springs Hotel ten days ago! Can you beat that for luck?

You would love this spot—the beauty of it, and the peace, unbroken by a single motor-car. I wish I had planned to stay longer. I have found a cabin on the lake side that appeals to me so I am sleeping there instead of in the main building, where the meals are served.

Hope you have a wonderful trip to Golden tomorrow.

Until Monday, at Lake Louise, and perhaps a little longer,

Yours,
Dan

Yoho Valley Lodge
Field, B.C.

Sunday noon, July 18

Dear Chief Dan No Hat:

The two Knights of the Camera have returned from Lake O'Hara bringing me your letter.

The reason for this note is that I found your Wapta–Lake Louise bus ticket that you will need tomorrow stuck between the pages of *Who Killed Cock Robin,* the story with which you were resting your mind before you left here. If you don't yet know that you haven't the ticket, cheer up—the operation is all over, and by the time you get to Lake Louise, I'll be there holding the ticket in my hand.

Try brushing your hair before you leave Lake Wapta; perhaps if you do the driver will trust you for the fare

[97]

till you get to the end of the trip.

I'm happy you find Lake O'Hara so beautiful. Bring back some lovely water colour sketches.

You may have all the O'Hara fish; I'm to see the inside of a roundhouse tomorrow, thanks to Mr. Ross, the likable factotum of Field Divisional Headquarters of the C.P.R. Now don't you wish you were here? But it is just as well you are not; there is a chance I may be able to borrow Mrs. McAndless's typewriter tonight and do a little work.

I'll be seeing you Monday, beside the "sky blue wa-ter."

Your loving Squaw

P.S. The ride to Golden was delightful.

P.P.S. If you get in a jam for something, telephone; I will jump on Spooks and bring whatever it is, riding like the wind to O'Hara, serene in the knowledge that if any old avalanche happened to be sliding around I would surely be rescued, just in the nick of time, by a Lone Ranger—I mean a Royal Canadian Mountie—with raisins in his pocket!

Your obedient Squaw

CHAPTER XI

ROUND-HOUSE AT FIELD

The Duchess's Diary

Monday night, July 19:—When I said good-bye to Mrs. McAndless this morning at Yoho Valley Lodge, I gave her for a souvenir some verses I wrote last night—and left her laughing.

MRS. McANDLESS'S TYPEWRITER

O, Yoho River and Yoho Pass
Are sights to remember, but mind this, my lass;
Not even the Yoho, where madly it foams,
Can buck, jump and skip over rocks as it roams,
Like Mrs. McAndless's typewriter.

You play with its keys and see on the white sheet
A line of black letters remarkably neat,
Then, right in the midst of your b-e-a-u-t-i-f-u-l
　　thought
She puts all four feet down and brings you up short—
Does Mrs. McAndless's typewriter!

That blessed machine is uncertain as marriage:
She will, and she won't! You may jiggle its carriage,

Try pushing and pulling, then hammer the keys—
Employ every method that's known to a tease;
In the end you'll give up and go climb to Twin Falls.
And next day, when again at the Lodge, within walls,
If you happen to touch it, she's off like a breeze;
Your thought in black letters goes marching with ease
On Mrs. McAndless's typewriter!

A half hour after leaving Yoho Valley Lodge this sunny morning, *en route* for Lake Louise, Mr. van Haitsma stopped his car near the railway station at Field, B.C. As we were parking, I was impressed by the sense that Field is sitting on the knees of Mount Burgess, whose head towers 8,000 (odd) feet above it. Now Jerry Van de Vusse, "Van," and I walked to the Divisional headquarters of the Canadian Pacific Railway and presented ourselves at the office of the kindly official, Mr. George M. Ross, who had previously invited us to meet his roundhouse.

After untangling himself from a telegraph instrument and giving a word here and there to others in his office, Mr. Ross welcomed us with a smile, of the sort they make out here in the high altitudes—clear, kind, and courteous. Then we all went out and started to walk through the railway yard, crossing tracks.

Standing on a siding was a huge locomotive, No. 5906. I stopped to look at it and was asked would I like to get into its cab. That was exactly what I wanted to do. Mr.

Mount Sir Donald

Ross gave me a hand up, and I managed to swing myself into the small space where an engineer handles great power. There I was, enjoying the sensation I'd wanted for years to have; I was gazing at a big panel full of dials and throttles, sitting in the engineer's seat, leaning out of a window, imagining myself responsible for the lives of a train-load of passengers!

As I prepared, with hands somewhat grimy, to descend from the cab to the ground, I saw on the floor of the cab of this 375-ton locomotive, a brass-bound tool box, and incised on its cover were the letters of a man's name. Instantly I wished for something to drop into the box that would puzzle its owner, "Mac," when he came back to get his tools. (One should always carry along in a pocket a few small "surprises," as well as an emergency ration of raisins. In my suitcase were little gifts to drop along the way of travel, but not a thing did I have at hand.)

Here are some items caught in the course of conversation as I walked with Mr. Ross to the roundhouse, and if anybody sees this, don't hold Mr. Ross responsible for what I say!

Coal is burned in locomotives from Montreal to Calgary, oil from Calgary to Vancouver—120 barrels of oil on an engine for a 250-mile run. The oil must be of the best quality. The engine cab, with draught between the two windows, is cooler than other parts of the train.

In the mountain area, where the driving is more difficult, a run of 125 miles is called an engineer's day.

In its cleanness and order the roundhouse was to me
fascinating, especially the engine room; and when I saw
a clock that shows three kinds of time—Atlantic, Mountain, and Pacific—I wanted a little one like it to have
at home. In the West, time is reckoned from one to
twenty-four hours, instead of A. M. and P. M. We looked
at an up-to-the-minute turntable, for swinging locomotives around, that was balanced on both ends instead
of only in the middle. We were shown how the sand for
traction is sifted twice, then thoroughly dried, and
finally blown up into storage places in the cars, ready
for an emergency. Beside the locomotives lined up ready
to go out, there were snow ploughs. One old plough Mr.
Ross showed us hadn't been out of the house in twelve
years, he said, when suddenly a few years ago a terrific
storm made it necessary to call out everything. This
old fellow went along and did a good job. The new
ploughs eat up the snow with amazing speed.

Mr. Ross's enthusiasm had touched our imaginations,
turning mere metal "into steel of empire," to use Mr.
Murray Gibbon's significant phrase.

As we said good-bye to him in his office, I noticed on
Mr. Ross's desk a pretty, old-fashioned bouquet of
pansies and sweet william.

CHAPTER XII

LAKE LOUISE AND MR. MARMOT

IF you have ever sat at a table for two beside a window in the dining-room of the Chateau, you'll feel again as you read this what the Duchess and I felt at breakfast on our first morning at Lake Louise. You will remember the high, wide windows, so clear one does not realize glass is between the tables and the tall spires of blue delphinium outside; rather, one seems to be out of doors gazing upon the peaks of Lefroy and Victoria mountains that tower 11,000 feet above their own reflections in this loveliest of lakes.

On the morning I speak of, delphinium and mountains were not all the picture upon which we gazed while enjoying what might be called a "pontifical" breakfast. There were yellow poppies that swept down terraces to meet emerald lawns, which in turn ran to the edge of the lake's blue waters, stopped by the mirrored likeness of dark forest, shining peaks, and snowy Victoria Glacier.

"It is the irony of Fate," exclaimed the Duchess, "that we should have left only three days of this trip for Lake Louise; I'd heard so much praise of it I was suspicious."

"But Duchess, you forget, we shall be coming to Louise again on our way to Moraine Lake, when we go with the Sky Line Hikers to Larch Valley, and also after the Pow Wow at the end of the Hike."

The Duchess, whose bump of location is not well developed, as I think I've remarked before, brightened visibly, as she said:

"Two more visits! Then I shall have time to get acquainted with the volumes on Alpine flowers—you know, the ones by Mrs. Walcott which were published by the Smithsonian Institution. At this altitude—what is it, fifty-six hundred feet?—I'm going to exercise my faculties on the level."

"Contrariwise, I've been fortifying myself with beefsteak because I'm about to follow a trail up to the Plain of the Six Glaciers."

"Six Glaciers," she murmured. "Sounds as though the trip would take a week. What shall you do for food?"

"By three o'clock I hope I shall have reached a tea house, where Joe says they serve a substantial snack."

" 'Substantial snack' is a contradiction of terms, Dan; I'll bet it means ham and eggs—than which there is no more redundant combination. Pig *or* chicken, yes; but pig *and* chicken—not for me. A roast of beef smothered in lamb stew would be equally attractive." Smiling at her I said as I polished off the last bit of steak:

"Remind me to try it sometime. When I sat down I was as hungry as the Twin Falls porcupine; now I'm prepared for any strain the day may bring." We arose, sauntered out of the dining-room, the Duchess asking as we passed down the wide stairs into the lobby, "Where does your trail begin?"

"Right here on the west shore of the lake, but I'm going to row to the other end and pick up the trail near the boat landing. Like to come along?"

"Theoretically yes; actually, I'm going to stretch out in one of those nice long chairs on the terrace, in the sun, within reach of the big telescope; once in awhile I may check up on your progress!" With a laugh she left me and I went down to the boat-house to see Joe.

Joe, one of the group of Swiss guides who live in the chalet on the grounds, has charge of boats, helps guide the mountain climbers in summer and guard the hotel property in winter. Among other things they do, the Swiss guides keep the hotel's great expanse of roof freed from heavy falls of snow.

After I had told Joe what I wished to do, he gave me one of his boats that rowed most easily—I didn't want a canoe—and I started off for a pull of about three miles.

Moving slowly upon the sapphire surface of Lake Louise I watched with intense pleasure the play of light and shadow upon the mountains that ran steeply down to its shores, losing count of time until I found myself at the landing. Tying the boat, I started walking up the trail, my back to the lake, and Mount Lefroy on my left. The glacier at the top of Lefroy looked as though one good push would send it hurtling into the valley below.

Pottering along, I found myself stopping frequently to look down at Lake Louise, set in the midst of dark pines. As I ascended, its colour seemed to change, and now was no longer sapphire-blue, but brilliant emerald-green. Further up, I came upon sight of a mountain torrent. Fed by the glaciers toward which I was hiking, it rushed whitely downward to the foot of Lefroy.

Suddenly around a bend in the trail above me came two fat men, coats over their arms, straw hats on the back of their heads:

"How much further to the hotel?" called the biggest man. Ignoring his question I called back, "Where have you been?"

"Up to the Tea House—about forty miles I should say," he answered, mopping his brow, as he and his companion reached me.

"In that case," I answered smiling, "it will be about sixty back to the Chateau." As they passed on down, the shorter man turned his head to say, "Gosh, distances fool you in these here mountains, don't they?"

"They sure do," I replied, knowing that the entire

distance from Chateau to Tea House was only about six miles.

The two weary walkers disappeared from the scene, and I went on up, wondering what they would tell their families when they got home. Before me now rose a great sheer cliff, and next it the wall of Victoria Glacier. Between them there is a narrow passage, called by the Alpine guides the Trap. Climbers to Mount Victoria have to pass through this opening, and they do so before sun-up. After the sun has risen there is always danger of snow slides coming off Mount Lefroy and Mount Victoria, and meeting in this place so well called the Trap. Gazing toward it now, I seemed to hear the Duchess saying, "But what makes people want to go through such places?"

Rounding a last turn in the trail I saw above me, off to the right, the Tea House. It proved to be another of the beautiful log structures which dot the National Parks. A group of hikers on an upper balcony waved to me and I joined them to find the views magnificent. Seating myself at a small table I lighted a pipe and took a few minutes' rest. By this time breakfast seemed something I had eaten months before.

Was there ever such a view as this? I was about to get out a map that would help me orient myself in relation to the great peaks and glaciers surrounding this small log house when a menu was placed before me on the table and a voice inquired, "Do you wish something to eat?"

I glanced at the card. Yes, there they were—Ham and Eggs! They dominated all the other things, and good they proved to be.

Refreshed, I went off to make a sketch, a record of the day, finally settling myself on a pile of rocks a few hundred yards from the Tea House.

At Emerald Lake I had been startled when I suddenly looked out of my window and into the eye of Mr. Moose, but that was nothing to what I felt a few minutes after I began to sketch in the Plain of the Six Glaciers. The feeling that crept over me here was the uncanny one that something was looking over my shoulder. Though I kept on working, there was no virtue in what I did, and at last, unable to bear the suspense any longer, I turned my head—and looked into the face of a whis-tling marmot!

The marmot sat at my elbow, watching as though he had a flair for art. I recognized him at once. Hadn't the Duchess and I, when at Manoir Richelieu, Murray Bay, often gazed at meal-time upon a portrait of a whistling marmot which had been painted by the great Audubon? Now here among the glaciers, marmot, in the flesh, and I had met.

I don't know why it is, but whenever I meet any of the native inhabitants of these Rocky Mountains I im-

Lake Louise and the Victoria Glacier

mediately wonder if they are carnivorous. It would have been so easy for my neighbour on the rock to take a piece out of my shoulder that involuntarily I jumped up. The marmot retreated. I sat down; marmot came back. Then I saw other marmots sitting around, each one curious about me and what I was doing on their preserve.

The sketch wasn't going well; I couldn't keep my mind on the work and on my furry friends at the same time. I gave up and, bidding the creatures good afternoon, started down the trail for home.

Everything was changed now, the mountains on the left were casting long violet shadows. When the waters of Lake Louise came into view they had changed again to shining sapphire-blue.

Half way down I met a young couple walking up. The girl, poor thing, had open strap sandals on her little feet, and the heels were two inches high. She was finding the going hard. About a hundred yards further on I was brought up short by the sight of a little creature sitting on a rock. I'd heard of it—that it was difficult to see—and here it was, the size of a mouse, and with enormous ears—a real rock rabbit, and I didn't have a camera with me!

At the landing I untied the boat and was about to step into it when I heard a shout and, turning in the direction of the voice, saw a chap I'd met at Lake O'Hara coming down the last bit of trail; he must have been behind me all the way.

"Want a ride?" I called and, coming up, he said:

"I'd love it—been hiking all day—over the trail from O'Hara." As we got into the boat he said, "Here, let me row; it's my arms that need exercise now."

So, in the evening light we skimmed home as if in a racing shell, over the placid surface of Lake Louise, I sitting in the stern, smoking a pipe, "to my great content."

CHAPTER XIII

FISHING: CONSOLATION LAKES

THE day after my trip to the Plain of the Six Glaciers I went down to the boat-house at Lake Louise, this time to talk fish. Most of Joe's boats were out on the lake, so he had time to smoke a pipe with me while answering my questions.

"People won't believe it," said Joe, "but fish are wise. For instance, the tourists thrash this lake every day, and few of them ever catch a good trout, while, as a matter of fact, the lake is full of fine fish—but they're wise." Getting up and going over to a box he had on a shelf: "I'll show you."

Taking something from the box Joe walked out onto the float and threw bits of it into the water. Gosh! what a sight. Great trout that I'll bet weighed up to five pounds instantly appeared, thrashing the water.

"There they are," said Joe, "but just try to get one of those beauties with a fly! As I said, they are wise."

I told Joe that I wanted to enjoy a day of good fishing, and that I had but one day left to do it in. Joe went into a huddle with himself.

[111]

"Tell you what," he said, "go over to Consolation Lakes and you'll get the limit. Drive over to the Valley of the Ten Peaks, leave your car there, then take the trail on the left. It's an easy walk of about three miles to the lakes."

I thanked him, and I didn't tell him poor old Sally was in a garage in Montreal; but on my way back to the Chateau I wondered how I was going to get to the Valley of the Ten Peaks.

As I hurried into the hotel, the pleasant assistant manager met me, saying: "You're the man I'm looking for. A Mr. Siegle from Seattle has just arrived and wants someone to go fishing with tomorrow." Lady Luck was with me. In a few minutes Mr. Siegle was found and agreed with pleasure that we should go in his car to Consolation Lakes.

When one talks to a golfer and learns that he is a three-handicap man, one knows what kind of a game he will play; when one talks to a fisherman and hears about waxed lines and greased lines, wet and dry flies, the rod for this and the rod for that, one knows what kind of fishing to expect. Siegle's equipment made mine look funny, and I felt like a golfer who has set out for a game with nothing but a driver, an iron, and a putter.

Next morning, a little after nine o'clock, Siegle and I took the road leading to the main highway and turned to the right at a sign which bore the words, Valley of the Ten Peaks. That word combination has a thrill in it.

The fine road wound up and up, giving us wonderful views, off to the left, of distant mountains veiled in blue haze. The eight miles were soon covered; then suddenly, around a bend in the road, soaring to high heaven, the great Peaks from which the valley gets its name came into view. The sun was in such a position that they appeared, one after another, as a great blue curtain; and at their base like a jewel gleamed Moraine Lake.

I could have remained at the bend of the road, satisfied to call it a day, gazing on the wonder of the scene and wishing I had brought water colours instead of a rod. But my companion's voice was saying, "Here we are— turn in; this is the camp ground."

I came back to earth and looking through some trees saw a group of tents and smoke rising from a camp-fire. The sight brought a thrill as there flashed into mind happy months the Duchess and I have spent under canvas in Eastern Canada.

Among the trees was a good-sized shelter built of logs; under it was a large community cook stove, surrounded at the moment of our arrival by a family that had just finished breakfast. As we got out of the car a tall young man, evidently the man of the family seated around the table, called out to us, "Going fishing?" Those two words drew us over to the speaker like a magnet, and in a moment the tall stranger was a companion. When we told him where we were going he said:

"Best fishing ground around. I've been here four days and have caught the limit every time I have been out. Wait till I get my shoes on," he said with excitement, "and I'll show you the way up the trail."

The man's dear old mother was clearing up the breakfast things, and called out: "Oh, what a boy my son is! All he wants to do is to go fishing." And she added, stuffing another log into the stove, "He always brings home such lovely fish."

"Isn't this a fine stove?" she asked, turning to me. "I keep it going all day." The thing in which she took so much pride was a concrete box about six feet long, two feet wide, and two feet high, with a cast iron top that covered the whole thing. One could cook by the yard on that stove, I thought, noticing that near by was a large stock of wood cut to fit. I saw at once why Mother found it easier to keep the fire going all day. One could camp with such a stove all the year round.

Son now had his boots on and led the way; we followed him, starting up the trail for a three-mile hike to the Consolation Lakes.

Son and Siegle talked the language of fishermen; I brought up the rear. One moment I felt excited over our guide's story of what we might expect when we reached the fishing-ground, and next I was wishing for my paint box. Going steadily forward, we soon found the trees

were thinning; then we emerged into a valley. Off in
the distance in an emerald-green setting I saw what
looked like a great sapphire—the lakes of Consolation.

The way was now rather marshy and we saw that a
wide stream was flowing from the lake nearest us.

"The best place to fish," called our tall young man,
"is on the right of the lake; we'll have to climb over
those rocks you see ahead. It's pretty hard going; watch
your step." I saw before us what at one time in the
far distant past had been part of the mountain that now
rose beside the lake. There must have been a million tons
of rocks in sizes anywhere from a peach basket to a
three-room cottage, scattered from the edge of the lake
for several hundred yards up the mountainside; and I
soon found out why we had been told to watch our
steps.

Never have I seen such chaos and utter desolation.
(But I haven't seen Spain since the champions of liberty
finished with it.) After some climbing and crawling I
established myself on a flat rock that jutted out into the
lake. About a hundred yards from me Siegle found a
spot that suited him; Tall Boy, seeking his favourite
place, kept on going until he was almost lost in the distance.

There was something wrong with my rig, for after
casting awhile all I had caught was one small trout.

"How are you getting on?" called Siegle. "I've got

five beauties."

"What are you using?" I called back to him.

"Dry fly," came the answer. And I had been trying to cast a wet fly against the wind that had arisen! Determined to see how Siegle did it, I crawled over to him, and just as I came up he said:

"See that shallow water out there that just about covers those rocks? That's where they are lying." I should as soon have thought of trying to cast a fly across the Hudson River as to have tried to reach that place, but as I watched, Siegle whipped his rod back and forth, then out shot the line. The fly lit as gracefully as a moth on the exact spot he had pointed out to me. Instantly there was a flash of silver spray as the trout struck.

In an hour we had caught the limit allowed—twenty trout—and we turned about and hiked back to the car. It had been a great day. I had seen the Consolation Lakes, Lake Moraine, and the Valley of the Ten Peaks which I shall never forget. Finis. And Glory to God!

Next morning I went down to the boat-house to tell Joe about my experience fishing at Consolation Lakes. (Talking things over with Joe was getting to be a habit.) After I had told him that dry flies were what caught all the fish, he said, laughing:

"You should have been here yesterday. After you left in the morning, a chap came along and asked me how much I charged for a boat. I told him and he took a

Consolation Lake

boat for an hour—said he thought he'd go fishing. 'Have
you got a rod?' I asked. 'Sure,' he said, and pulled out
a little steel contraption that cost about a dollar, with a
reel on it about the size of a half dollar and a fly that
looked as though moths had been eating it. Well, I gave
him a boat and off he went.

"I was busy getting boats ready for people up at the
Chateau when the chap with the moth-eaten fly comes
back. I looked at my watch and saw he'd been gone only
about half an hour.

" 'Have any luck?' I called, as I went out to meet him.

" 'Darned small fish you got in this lake,' says he, and
flops a seven-and-a-half-pound trout out onto the float
at my feet."

CHAPTER XIV

APRICOTS, PRUNES, AND RAISINS

AFTER two weeks spent in visiting Emerald Lake, Yoho Valley Lodge, Lake O'Hara (I alone), and finally Lake Louise, the Duchess and I, knowing the road to be excellent, chose to return to Banff by a special motor bus scheduled to leave Chateau Lake Louise at seven o'clock on the morning of July 23. This would get us to Banff by nine o'clock, an hour before the first ceremony of Indian Days.

The morning was cool, the sun reluctant to come out from between clouds. As soon as the bus drove up to the Chateau (one with no top and plenty of blankets) eight of us took our places, the Duchess immediately behind the driver and I, as it happened, beside him. Being so near the front we were somewhat protected by the windshield, but the couples behind us got a steady buffeting of air as soon as the bus started down the long incline to Lake Louise Station. Our young driver wore no extra coat, no sweater. I could sense the Duchess getting uneasy about him, so I wasn't surprised when she leaned forward and asked, "Aren't you cold?"

Slightly turning his head he replied, "I rushed off in a hurry without my coat."

"And breakfast?" asked the Duchess.

"I didn't have time to eat," replied the young man. Then to my surprise I heard the Duchess say to me:

"Feel in your left coat pocket, Dan—you'll find a package of dried fruit. Feed him." I burst out laughing. Upon pulling out and unwrapping the package, I saw an assortment of dried apricots, prunes and figs.

"Well, I'll be jiggered, Duchess," I said. "Is this the fruit you were so bent upon buying in Montreal?"

"It is part of it," she answered. "I knew that sometime, somewhere, when away from a source of supply, there would be need for food; and now, here is this young man perishing with hunger. You do like these nice chewy dried fruits, don't you?" she asked of the smiling bus driver.

"Sure," he chirped; so, with the bus rolling along at a good clip through spruce woods of the Rocky Mountains, and my gaze upon the green valley of the Bow, I handed the twenty-year-old beside me, now a fig, now a prune, now an apricot, from the store that, unknown to me, the Duchess had cached in a pocket of my overcoat.

As the Brewster bus travelled on its descending way past Coral Creek, there was a moment's view of the Ten Peaks. . . . A moment later, out of the corner of my eye I saw the Duchess handing a large silk muffler over the back of her seat to a perishing male whose coat collar was yawning to the breezes, and heard her say:

"Do please take this—I have two. The wind is blowing straight down your neck; tie up your collar with it." A quick glance toward the back seats showed me that the ladies who had carelessly stepped into an open bus for a 34-mile drive wearing wide-brimmed hats, with no visible means of support, now looked pinched and cold as they sat clutching their head-gear. The attentive driver chose this moment to point out to us Storm Mountain, explaining that the mountain was so named because it had a habit of wearing a cloud on its head when a storm was brewing in Kicking Horse Valley.

The Duchess leaned forward and whispered in my left ear, "I'd rather wear a cloud than a wide-brimmed hat!"

Near Castle Mountain Government Camp, we paused a moment to watch a big brown bear in the woodland above the road. It was quite undisturbed by our presence. I fed the driver more fruit. We drove along and passed an old smelting oven. There was once a silver mine in this vicinity; years ago the buildings and all the workers were removed to Golden—all, that is, except one man. He stayed on, and now, very old, lives here all alone. In telling me this, the driver also pointed out in the dis-

tance Pilot Mountain, and added that the base of Castle
Mountain, which the bus was then skirting, is 11 miles
long. . . . The three A's that mean good accommodation for motorists was on the sign of Johnston Canyon
Bungalow Camp, 16 miles from Banff, when we stopped
there to rearrange blankets. During a moment of general
conversation, I saw the Duchess offering her extra coat
to one of the blue-nosed ladies, saying with a laugh:

"Slip this on. I always carry more than I shall need
for myself when travelling. You can give it back to me
at Banff Springs Hotel."

Now, with Mount Edith towering above it, the steep
flank of the Sawback Range hemmed in our road on
the left. We saw plainly the dark aperture of Hole-in-
the-Wall Mountain and, looking at it, I remembered the
story I had heard about a guide who told a credulous
tourist that the hole was the back entrance to Banff
Springs Hotel.

Along the reaches of Vermilion Lakes we stopped to
see the Beaver Huts. Those little brown beavers leave
beauty, as we think of it, out of their calculations, but
their intelligence and capacity for work are certainly
amazing. At this point in our trip I handed to the driver
the final fig of the Duchess's secret store.

Thanks to a rising sun and a lowered altitude (of 500
feet) the temperature was much warmer, though the

passengers on the back seats seemed not to be aware of it until we were driving into the courtyard of Banff Springs Hotel. Then, the sight of its terraced and towered beauty assuring them of comfort, they released their hats, threw back their wraps and, as the invigorated young driver drew his motor coach up to the wide steps of the hotel portico, the ladies, assisted by a uniformed doorman, stepped forth with smiles into their native element.

It was with real pleasure that we again found ourselves in the hotel, being welcomed by the agreeable staff; by charming Miss Whyte, unfailingly cheerful fountain-head of information for every eager visitor; by Miss McGowan, peerless hostess. When, again in our apartment, the Duchess and I gazed from its windows at the matchless expanse of Bow River Valley and all its ranging mountains, we agreed that, while the unique places we had been visiting could not properly be compared with one another, nothing we had seen or enjoyed during our two weeks' trip had diminished the glamorous charm of Banff.

We were still looking out of the windows when she exclaimed, "Mercy! Dan, there's just time to get to the village if we want to see the Indian chiefs come riding over Banff bridge in full regalia."

Five minutes later we were in the lobby again. Instantly a pleasant young man rushed up to us, saying:

"I've been watching for you both; you are to ride in the press car to the village. This way please." Once more the Duchess and I were off for a big day.

CHAPTER XV

INDIAN DAYS AT BANFF

WITH a swing of the wheel the driver of the press car
whirled us around the courtyard of Banff Springs Hotel,
out past the Corral and the Athletic Grounds, and then,
stepping on the gas, he speeded into the village as though
on assignment to cover the coronation of George the
Sixth. In three minutes the car was parked, and those
camera boys, lugging their machines, scattered to posi-
tions among a crowd of white men and Indians that
filled the bridge from side to side of Bow River.

Near the bridgehead, watching with alert eyes from
under the brims of their Stetson hats, two Royal Canadian Mounties in red coats and black breeches sat erect
on shining chestnut horses that stood perfectly quiet
amid the pressing, chattering sightseers.

Standing for a moment somewhat above the crowd,
the Duchess and I agreed that the scene below us on the
bridge was worth having left Lake Louise to see, which
is saying a lot. Then we went down into the throng of
people on Bow Bridge, shouldering our way along in
friendly fashion, till we got close to the resplendent

Indians, who were sitting motionless, their immobile faces as keen in line as the crags of their native mountains.

Indian chiefs, in white doeskin coats and trousers richly embroidered in coloured beads, were lined up, single file, on pinto ponies decorated for the occasion in embroidered trappings that suggested the days of jousts and tournaments. War bonnets of black-tipped white feathers crowned the head and cascaded down the back of every Stony, Cree, Blackfoot, Blood and Piegan chief in the procession that sunny morning. It was the feathers, stirring in the wind from the mountains, that gave accent and movement to the whole picture. In my mind I shall always see those Indian heads as I saw them that day, etched by the sun on a bluish background of towering mountains.

Suddenly I turned and saw that the Duchess had gone off on her own; she was talking with Mr. and Mrs. Carl Rungius. Rungius and I are fellow members of the National Academy of Design, in New York, who hadn't seen each other in years until the night of our arrival in Banff. Then Mrs. Rungius's invitation to spend our first evening with them, at their summer home here, brought us together again and gave a warm and friendly start to our Western adventure. That was the first expression of many which put us in debt to the Rungius' generosity, and which, among other good things, brought us the

[125]

acquaintance of that unique couple, Lieutenant Colonel and Mrs. P. A. Moore. Without the Moores, Banff, Alberta and British Columbia—yes, the entire Rocky Mountain area—could scarcely function. An afternoon party at the Moores' house, filled, as it proved to be, with Indian treasures and the spirit of hospitality, has been set down in the Duchess's Golden Book among the hours that time cannot destroy.

Now, as I looked about, over the heads of the crowd on Bow Bridge, I caught sight of Dan McCowan, the naturalist and lecturer, with his charming wife. Dan had his camera with him and was talking earnestly to Mr. R. H. Palenske of Chicago, who is the President of The Trail Riders of the Canadian Rockies.

As camera men near me were busy photographing the handsome costumes of certain chiefs whom they had persuaded to dismount for a moment, there came a stir. The Mounties, in their scarlet tunics, began to clear a way so that the procession of Indians might move along to its objective—the Banff Springs Hotel courtyard. At that moment the Duchess appeared at my elbow.

"Come on, Dan," she said, "the car is going back at once; the camera men want to get to the hotel ahead of the procession."

A few minutes later our car swung into the hotel courtyard on two wheels and came to an abrupt stop in front of a crowd assembled to welcome Indians.

"It is too bad to disappoint them," remarked the Duchess, looking happily at our audience as she and the rest of us jumped out of the car and hurried up the steps of the porch past ranks of waiting sightseers, "but hasn't it been fun—this being whirled about?"

An hour later, when the procession of Indian chiefs and, at the rear, their squaws, had reached the courtyard of Banff Springs Hotel, the annual ceremonies and giving of prizes took place before guests assembled on the hotel's wide porch.

Mr. Norman Luxton, a fine looking man who has spent his life among the Indians and who was in charge of the program, made a short speech relating to this anniversary of the signing of a treaty by the Five Indian Nations; then he awarded prizes for various accomplishments, introducing to the audience each chief, who responded politely with a few words. The prizes themselves, consisting of silver money, together with pipes, were given to each mounted chief by a pretty blond girl who walked from one to another, lifting their presents up to them with a slim white hand.

A highbred poise marked many of the chiefs, who received their gifts with a casual grace. Of course all the pipes had been smoked before they were given, "to make them good."

These prizes and gifts to the Indian chiefs and to their squaws are provided by the Canadian Pacific Railway and the Banff Springs Hotel, as are the great trays of fruit, chocolate and cigarettes which were borne about to every Indian rider in the courtyard by waiters of the hotel.

One old chief who found it difficult to hold in his gauntletted hands an orange, a chocolate bar and a pipe, as well as the reins of his horse, slipped the pipe up under the embroidered band of his feathered head-dress and into its felt crown, from which depended two long bands of skilfully arranged eagle feathers. Another chief, upon receiving his gifts, drew up an elaborately embroidered pouch which hung from his saddle and stuffed everything into that.

The Indians have what I think is a delightful custom; they bestow a new name upon a man when he has accomplished something notable. On this occasion the Blackfoot Tribe, in the person of their chief, bestowed a new name on Mr. Luxton, their good friend, and gave him a pair of embroidered gauntlets. Mr. Luxton responded happily when he learned that his name had been changed by the Indians to White Eagle.

The Duchess whispered to me as we listened to this part of the program: "Why don't we white people do that, Dan? There is many a man who would count it as good as a new lease of life to be given a new name."

The Duchess's Diary

Midnight, Sunday, July 25:—While everything is vivid in my mind I want to write down what Dan and I saw and heard tonight.

Hurrying back from Banff Village to the Indian Concert due to start at seven o'clock, Dan and I cut across the Athletic Field adjoining Banff Springs Hotel to the grand stand set against rising land. Already several hundred people were seated, awaiting the beginning of a program of songs and dances to be performed by members of the Stony, Blackfoot, Sarcee, Blood and Piegan Tribes. For a moment we feared there were no seats left, but we managed to find two places on a bench near the top of the stand; from there we looked over the heads of the audience down into a grassy enclosure which tonight was the "stage."

At the left of the enclosure, posed against dark green of encircling spruce trees, sat a group of Indian squaws, their head coverings and shawls of brilliant colours suggesting exotic bloom in the midst of a northern scene.

At the right of the grassy stage, Indian braves, young, and older, stood in colourful costumes, waiting to perform the songs and dances of their aboriginal race.

Over the heads of an audience of sophisticated white men and women, above and beyond the primitive figures of Indians encircled by forest trees, we gazed far off to

[129]

where in the sunset sky clouds hung motionless in glory. It was the moment of consecration in the diurnal ritual of Light.

The sun sank below the jagged peaks of distant ranging mountains and dark forest. While gold was still shining around the edges of clouds in the western sky, the program began.

Mr. Norman K. Luxton was master of ceremonies, and, after an interesting opening speech about the Indians he knows so well, he introduced Chief Yellow Horn of the Blackfoot Tribe, and Chief Turn-up-Nose, a Piegan, who in turn made short addresses to the audience. Seen in the light of history, how strange, I thought, that hundreds of friendly whites should be listening politely to friendly words spoken by red men. That we and they were enjoying an evening together, for mutual enlightenment, is due in no small measure to the management of Banff Springs Hotel, and to Mr. Luxton's labours of many years on behalf of the Indians.

Now the entertainment began, with Joshua Wildman who told us about the Drum Dance Song, and then it was sung for us in the Stony language by a guest artist—Edgar Onespot of the Sarcee Reservation. Following this, tall Indian men in colourful costumes performed the Deer Dance; they were led by Medicine Man Blind Eagle (Paul Amos). It was an amazing sight. I was too much absorbed to write any notes at the time and now I cannot describe it. The squaws watched their men folk perform this dance with what seemed intense interest.

A chorus followed, sung in the Stony language by men who as children fifty years ago learned its music from the early missionaries. It gave me strange feelings.

To the singing of the traditional Owl Song the Owl Dance was performed and awakened in me a desire to know about the Indian arts.

Chief David Bearspaw, whom I saw in the Calgary parade, figured in a Night Song and its Dance, as did also Teddy Fly.

There were many types of Indians among the performers. One dignified figure of a man had been on the Morley Reservation since 1885; others were akin to our present day college youth.

The number that meant the most to me was an ancient song of which there is no written record; it has been handed down orally from father to son, and is called "Walking Alone." The name is enough to make poetic goose flesh rise on one's skin; to have heard it was an experience. So strangely beautiful was the rhythm that the whole audience, to say nothing of ourselves, was moved to applause as George McLean and Walking Buffalo sang the melodic meditation. "Walking Alone" is the oldest song known to any of the Five Tribes.

With dramatic contrast, "Walking Alone" was followed by a war dance. Drums sounding, and all the performers in beautiful feather war bonnets and other symbolic details of dress, twenty or more Indians formed a long cue and, with marked and stirring rhythm, danced single file the traditional steps that long ago meant trouble for the white man, and today, his entertainment.

In the moving line of dancers I noted particularly a handsome chief, One-Green-Grasshopper; beside him was a tiny boy, doubtless a son, who imitated his every step, keeping perfect time. Soon the progress of the dance brought these two nearer, and I saw that, like all others, the little boy was wearing bells on his legs, but that, unlike the others, his head-dress terminated in a striking imitation of insect antennae. ("The boy's mother," I thought to myself, "has taken great pains with his costume.") Soon the circling line brought man and boy to a place opposite the centre of the grand stand, where they were visible to everyone. And there, with bells jingling bravely, and tiny feet moving swiftly to the ancient impulse, the baby warrior put on such a spot of dancing that the whole grand stand rose in applause. Little Two-Green-Grasshopper stole the show!

There followed a half dozen short numbers, including a solo Chicken Dance with Arrows. By this time darkness began to settle upon the scene, and Johnny Small Eye brought the program to an end by singing for us "Home on the Range."

It had been an impressive evening. Now the audience rose to leave. At Mr. Luxton's invitation many persons, including ourselves, went down into the grassy enclosure and mingled with the artists of the evening.

After a few minutes of tentative communication with some of the chiefs (one could not call it "talking") Dan and I joined everyone present in holding hands with the Indians and hopping around in a good-night friendly dance. I can truthfully say that when I felt my hands being held by the strangely soft hands of two savage looking chiefs in beaded buckskin and feathers, and for some minutes actually danced with them, I experienced one of the most confusing and memorable sensations of my life.

CHAPTER XVI

KANANASKIS RANCH

AMONG the pioneer families that opened Western Canada to the world were the Brewsters. Today their name is familiar to every visitor to Alberta and British Columbia, because the descendants of the first Brewsters are now the owners of inns, ranches and transport companies that minister to the comfort and pleasure of the public.

When the Indian Days at Banff were ended, Dan and I found ourselves with nothing particular to do from Monday until Friday, July 30, when the big Trail Ride would begin.

"Why not go down to Claude Brewster's ranch near Seebe?" said Dan. "We could do some riding and harden up for the trail."

"A good idea," I replied. "Come on; let's talk with Miss Whyte." Now I'll wager that, in the course of a season at Banff Springs Hotel, not one person out of the hundreds that daily pass through its corridors, rest in its lounges, and sit entranced upon its terraces, ever fails to stop at the Information Desk and ask a question of

Indian Days at Banff, Alberta

Dorothy Whyte. The truth of the matter is that if you ask Miss Whyte one question you're lost—delightfully. Having once experienced her capacity to turn the beam of wisdom upon your particular problem and give you instantly the answer—not mere answer, but dependable information wrapped in a smile and tied around with a silver thread of personal interest—you go away only to return, again and again, it is all so pleasant.

On this Monday morning, Dan and I, by now Whyte addicts, sank into chairs near her desk and asked about Kananaskis Ranch.

"If you'll go to the lobby now," she said, "you'll find Mr. Claude Brewster there. Talk to him about going. All the rooms at his ranch house may have been taken, but if he can accommodate you it would be a wise move on your part to go to Kananaskis. Each of you would have your own horse for the duration of your visit, which you could retain for the five days of the Ride; and it's a great comfort, when you are out for rough riding, to know your horse."

That is the way it came about that Dan and I found ourselves alighting from a bus at cross-roads near Seebe about half past nine o'clock on Monday night, July 26, and saw Claude Brewster waiting for us.

Kananaskis Ranch, Tuesday, July 27. Afternoon:—I'm sitting in a cool shadow on the long open veranda at the back of this ranch house. Wild heliotrope is scenting the air with sweetness as I gaze out upon the sun-filled valley of Bow River. Far beyond the river's banks, rising against the whole arc of the southern sky from east to west, I see the forested or stony peaks of mountains.

Dan and I arrived here from Banff last night about half past nine, and we had our first ride this morning. There are sixteen agreeable young men and women here. The Brewsters are considerate of everyone's comfort, and they give us good meals and plenty of food. The guides are expert and the horses everything they should be, so what more could one ask of a "Dude Ranch"?

Before I write more about today I want to jot down incidents of yesterday.

We were met at the door of this house last night by Claude Brewster's mother, called affectionately, by everybody, Missy—a girlish grandmother, slim as a poplar, who took us into a homelike living-room where a fire was burning on the hearth. While we were talking, four guests came in from an evening ride and joined us. Shortly after, someone laughingly remarked that to-morrow would be another day and started off to bed. We were taken upstairs.

As we walked into our room, the sight of Hudson Bay blankets on the beds, with their black and yellow stripes, gave me pleasure. Through open windows the clear night showed a quiet river and, beyond its far, spruce-clad shore, dominant mountains in a serene sky.

This morning, Dan was down before me. I hadn't an idea whether to dress for a cold or a warm day, but got into riding togs and ran downstairs to a jolly breakfast. At the foot of the stairs I saw a big blackboard on which was chalked a schedule of the day's rides, and signed my name under the one to start at ten o'clock.

It was fun seeing the whole crowd at breakfast in the sunny dining-room. I ultimately learned that they hailed from as far away as England (Miss Sylvia Stevenson, novelist, of London, and her brother, Professor Arthur Stevenson, of Toronto), from New York, Philadelphia and Washington, D.C.; from Eastern and Western States, and from many parts of Canada, they had come to ride in the Canadian Rockies.

As the hour for the first ride approached, Dan and I walked up a woodsy path to the corral. Guides were mounting the riders, while a lot of fine horses in the corral stood looking eager for something to happen to them. Olie, a young Norwegian guide, mounted me on a pinto Indian pony, saying with a smile, "Scottie is steady and quiet; you'll like him." I thought of Brownie, at Yoho Lodge, and hoped this brown and white little creature might prove half as well adapted to my ignorance. Dan was given a big handsome bay named Baldy that would have been in his proper setting on the bridle path in Central Park, New York.

In the course of the morning ride, Scottie showed himself to be the horse I needed, and it cheered me immensely to know I was going to have him for the five days of the Trail Ride. Dan was kept busy reining Baldy in; the horse wanted to race and be always first in the line. "Not so good for the Trail Ride," I thought to myself, and still am thinking.

On the ride this morning ten of us rode out and returned by way of the great Kananaskis Falls in Bow River. This meant passing the power plant and riding over the locks that harness the waters. There were open spaces in the bridgelike top of the locks which the horses had to step across while making their way along; the roaring, foaming masses of water plunging beneath their feet—and mine—were visible. "Does Olic know how green I am?" I wondered. But the horses kept their heads, and our heads didn't matter, all went well.

Wednesday night:—Sixteen of us rode all this morning, stopped at noon beside a river, built a fire and had hot coffee with our sandwich luncheon. Afterward we rode home, getting to the ranch about four o'clock. We have seen interesting country these two days.

The Kananaskis Ranch boys put on a rodeo of their own, Tuesday night, for the entertainment of the guests; and it must have been a good show, because I felt shudders, watching the wild doings of men and animals. The next evening Colonel and Mrs. Moore came down from Banff for supper, and afterward showed to the assembled crowd beautiful movies taken by themselves on a trip to the Columbia Ice Fields. Later we had music; the guides came in and sang songs to guitar accompaniment.

By Thursday morning Dan and I had stored up enough memories to make us feel we had been at the ranch a month, and we were glad so many from there would be companions on the Trail Ride. All the horses from the ranch were to be driven to Banff (30 miles) on Thursday, so they would have a night's rest before starting for the mountains Friday morning. A few of the guests were staying on at the ranch; the rest of us packed and prepared to take the morning train.

Besides the ones I've already mentioned, there will be, riding to Mount Assiniboine, three young women from Buffalo, N.Y., friends, good riders, and jolly; charming Mary Downing and her friend Lucile Tucker, both from Kansas City, Missouri; Miss Ida Sandman of New York, an excellent rider and member of the Council of the Trail Riders' Association.

Claude Brewster drove us to Seebe station and prepared to flag the transcontinental train as casually as though there were nothing on his mind, when in reality, he had ahead of him all the provisioning of sixty persons for five days, away from a base of supplies.

Far down the track we saw the train coming; the flag was waved, and our old friend, *The Dominion,* slowed its length to a stop at the platform. Amid friendly good-byes from Claude Brewster and his two young sons, in big Western hats, we all boarded the train. Again Dan and I were going west. In an hour we were in Banff.

July 30, 8:45 A. M.:—This day, so long looked forward to, has arrived, and the sun is shining! Dan and I are all agog. We got up early, packed the things chosen last night as being indispensable, and have left the rest of our belongings in care of this hotel. Our duffle bags have already been taken, with those of the other riders who have been staying here. There will be fifty-five horses for the members and guests of the Association, aside from those used by the guides and camp workers; and a pack train of nearly as many more horses. Imagine! A company of cavalry in line! When I think of the work it will require to transport, pack, and unpack everything for the maintenance and comfort of so many people for five days and nights, I begin to think I have never done anything in my life.

The only equipment Dan and I have for this adventure in riding mountain trails is good health and a capacity to adapt ourselves to circumstances. We know nothing about riding and are "soft." We should have had a week's riding at Kananaskis Ranch. I've made up my

[140]

mind to keep a place in the line near a good rider, and then I shall watch him or her, and do as he does, unless my own judgment rebels. I wouldn't be able to follow the Angel Gabriel if my judgment told me an action were unwise.

Oh! Dan is calling from the doorway. He says, "Hurry up, Duchess; the motor bus has come that is to take us to Sundance Canyon where the horses are waiting!" Heigh Ho!

CHAPTER XVII

TRAIL RIDE TO MOUNT ASSINIBOINE

The Duchess's Diary

A SPECIAL motor bus carried all of us Trail Riders to Sundance Canyon and stopped in the midst of a crowd of men and women dressed for hard riding who had arrived before us. On each side of the road horses were tethered among the trees, and there was an air of excitement over the sunlit scene. Greeting and meeting one another among the fifty or more gathered there, while looking for our horses, took a few minutes. When I discovered my Scottie and Olie the guide from Kananaskis Ranch, Olie's smile, as he looked to the cinching of my saddle and mounted me, smoothed away my doubts. Dan too found his big horse and, mounting, rode out onto the wide road where a half dozen of us stood ready to go.

Without a word from us our horses began to trot along. Scottie trotting! I could hardly believe it. A switch had been necessary at the ranch to urge him forward. No doubt a horse enjoys fresh scenes as much as a person; anyway, Scottie and I were set to enjoy the day. I soon discovered that it mattered greatly what horse was ahead of him; he always wanted to be near the big roan from Kananaskis.

Scottie was a fast walker, and that is a golden virtue in a horse you'll be sitting on five days. Altogether I was contented as to my horse; I found myself wishing Dan were riding an Indian pony. Somehow, I distrusted his big bay.

The three young women from Buffalo were right ahead of me as we moved along through woodland where, now and then, a beautiful vista was revealed by a turn in the road. We came to a place where a stream poured down from heights. Our horses, one after the other, with no word from us, veered aside and, going down to the bank, crowded along the edge and drank deep of the clear waters. Scottie, I thought, must be awfully dry, or he is wise and knows it will be a long time between drinks. Out we came from the trodden bank, and up to the hard surface again.

Now, roadway was left behind; we took to a narrow trail that ascended sharply, and the horses began digging in. At the end of an hour they stopped to drink from another stream. In getting back on the trail, I found myself just behind Carl Rungius, the artist, and saw ahead of him Mr. Palenske, the president of the Trail Riders, and Colonel Moore, an ex-president. At this mo-

[143]

ment raindrops began falling out of a lowering sky, and I recalled that, when we had been standing in sunshine at Banff, Mr. Rungius had looked up at the sky and remarked to my astonishment, "It looks like rain today."

Along and along. Olie rode up from the other end of the line to see how I was doing. The raindrops fell more steadily. Suddenly Mr. Rungius, riding ahead of me, put one hand behind him, pulled loose the leather thongs that fastened a raincoat to his saddle, and skilfully slipped the coat on. A second later, Mr. Palenske, ahead of him, went through exactly the same actions. Not a bad idea, I thought, and proceeded in like manner to get into a silly affair of waterproofed silk, wishing I had brought something big and businesslike to keep me dry. As I was struggling into the sleeves, I saw in my mind each of the long line of riders behind me, one after another, in succession, like a ballet routine, slipping their arms into raincoats, and I wished I could turn completely around to see it happening.

A little past noon the head of the cavalcade reached a glade beside Brewster Creek. I saw the pack horses that had left Banff before us tethered to trees. As the three score riders poured into the shrubby bottom, each one dismounted, tethered his horse and, after stretching and walking a bit, found a place near the fire over which boilers of water were heating. The rain had ceased. Pretty Mrs. Claude Brewster kept an eye on the lunch-

eon arrangement, and soon we were enjoying sandwiches, fruit and good hot tea and coffee. Mrs. Brewster
rode a beautiful black horse as though she were part of
it, and her littlest son, wearing a wide-brimmed hat and
riding a quick little pony, had shown himself that morning to be quite the equal of any of the grown-ups.

We took to the horses again a little after two o'clock,
this time well buttoned up against the weather, for rain
was falling. How I blessed Mrs. Carl Rungius for her
beautifully warm Hudson Bay blanket coat she had insisted I take with me on this ride through the mountains.
Without it, I should have perished a dozen times. With it,
I never once was chilled through. In the course of the next
four days it was always on my back, or at night added
warmth to my sleeping-bag. Wet boots (with wool
socks inside them) had no power for ill, in company
with the embracing warmth of that blanket coat.

The pack horses had gone on ahead of our horses; in
all there were a good hundred and twenty in line on the
narrow trail that led to Brewster Creek Ranger's Cabin,
near which an encampment would be made for the
night. Harder and harder the rain beat down upon us;
we took it in the face, I for one not minding because I
was warm. The trail became a matter of bogs, fallen tree
trunks, piled rocks, or stony stream beds. The whole
adventure being new to me, I accepted every incident as
just another and, finding I could trust Scottie, remained

undisturbed. One really travelled alone, for the man ahead, with his horse, was lost to speech, and the man on the horse behind one was as though he were not.

When Scottie and I accomplished what seemed to me a rather sporty number, I'd take a long breath and say, "Well, that's done; there can't be another like that." And there never was, because the next one was always worse. The harder the trail became and the more the distance between the horses increased, the more eager was Scottie to trot (how pathetic is the horse's fear of being alone); his motions, under the circumstances, were not exactly gliding. I blessed more and more, as the afternoon drew on toward five o'clock, a thirty-cent kapok pillow I had bought in Banff and, defying ridicule, had anchored by stout shoelaces to the horn of my saddle, at half past nine in the morning. To it I owed a sense of well-being and warmth. That night when strong men asked me with tears how I fared, adding that they were physically ruined, I smiled and told them thirty cents' worth of kapok would have enabled them to sit comfortably down to supper.

It was after five o'clock when out of grey mist loomed a grove of great trees with ruddy trunks rising straight up to rich green leafage—Englemann spruce! The sight brought refreshment to every sense. Riding into the grove between the great trunks of the trees, I caught sight of a newly built corral, and beyond, through the leafage, white cones of tepees rising in a pattern that took my mind back to the Indian encampment at Banff seen in the moonlight seven nights ago.

Camp workers were everywhere at once, unpacking horses, helping riders to find their quarters and putting into their hands the right duffle, hurrying to get all settled before darkness should fall. I marvelled at the guides' endurance and good nature.

Dan, whom I had scarcely seen all day, came to me beaming and said he had found a pup tent set up on an absolutely dry spot of earth and there he was going to spread his sleeping-bag and call it home. "And don't tell me to put boughs under it," he added, to my distress, "because I've plenty of blankets." However, when he wasn't looking, I sneaked into that pup tent and put a ground sheet under the sleeping-bag, and he never knew the difference.

In the tepee to which I was assigned, with two other ladies, I laid my sleeping-bag on spruce boughs that had been cut and piled, ready for use.

Skies suddenly cleared about nine o'clock, and a half hour later I slipped into my sleeping-bag and lay looking up at a star that seemed to be looking straight down at me; marvelling, until I fell asleep, that a tepee could be so comfortable a place to spend the night. Before starting on this ride I had asked a seasoned Westerner what one did about undressing when rough riding. He replied, "Well, I take off my boots." Acting on this suggestion, with certain feminine additions and improvements, I made out very well.

Blue sky burning through the tepee's open top waked me and my companions before six o'clock of our second day. And never shall I forget the beauty of that morning. Quickly polishing my face with alcohol, then cold cream, I topped off with a dash of comforting powder and stepped forth into an enchanting world.

White tepees like mushrooms rested in the green of a watered glade. Behind us on the west a green flank of mountain, high upon which our horses were grazing, rose steeply to the sky. A quarter of a mile from where I stood Brewster Creek wound through the green bottom, beside it cook tents and fires. Over the peaks of the eastern mountains the sun was not yet visible, but radiance of golden light filled all the scene.

Dan emerged from his pup tent and joined me. We walked to the stream where we dabbled our hands and faces. Then we sauntered to the grub tent, first customers of the day. While we were enjoying the bacon, pancakes and coffee, our cook told us the thermometer at that moment was nearly zero, and that the case of eggs he had expected to cook for breakfast were frozen hard, couldn't be used. The air was so dry Dan and I had not been conscious of the cold, but I recalled that the cup of water I had placed near me in the tepee last

*Brewster Creek Camp, Trail Riders of the
Canadian Rockies, 1937*

night had been frozen stiff this morning when I wanted to have a drink.

As we turned to walk back toward the encampment, the sight of smoke pouring out of the tops of the clustered tepees into the sunlight was something to remember.

When everyone had finished breakfast, the scene began to stir with action. Duffle was piled where the packers could get it; tepees disappeared as their white canvas was taken from the poles, folded and laid upon horses; men and women hunted up their horses, seeing that the saddles belonged to them. At last, with raincoats and small bags fastened to our saddles, the whole company was mounted and gathered near the stream, awaiting the word to start. It was again about nine-thirty A. M. when, the president and his officers leading the way, our cavalcade rode away from the encampment along a trail that at once went steeply up, first through forest of Englemann spruce and other fine trees, the horses plodding unconcernedly up and up until we came out upon upper reaches of shale, then winding along steep sides where the trail became a succession of narrow ledges, rounding shoulder after shoulder of stony mountains. Below the feet of our horses the depths were so remote I formed a habit of looking directly into the shale that was so close on my right I could touch it. Very gradually the distant bottom seemed to come up to meet us as the long line of horses wound slowly through Citadel Pass. At the summit, a Fox Movietone photographer took pictures of us as we rode through the pass. Snow flakes were falling. It was *cold* and everybody looked cold.

From the summit there was a gorgeous view. Moving on again, we were faced by what seemed to me a terrific descent. Along with the others I made the grade, and at the bottom we all pulled up to let the pack horses, who were behind us, go through. Here cameras were brought into action and we all did a little visiting on foot or on horseback. Then, with the pack train before us out of sight, we all moved forward.

About noon we reached the north fork of Bryant Creek and, riding up a high slope above it, dismounted and tied our good beasts to the bushes and trees. Reclining in sunshine upon the hillside we all luxuriated in the sense of warmth and scene, as below us cooks built a big fire and started heating the boilers. In due course we drank hot coffee and ate our luncheon with relish. Suddenly, as we were finishing, the sky clouded over, the wind grew strong.

It was time to be going; we went to our horses and began to untether them. But, a thing happened.

With a hand on Scottie to swing myself into the saddle I felt him tremble. Startled, I glanced around. Dan's big half-thoroughbred, ears pointing forward, seemed to be having an ague. Every pony near me showed signs of strong excitement. Why? In the second of taking my seat on Scottie's back and facing him about, I heard a distant sound that set every horse in our company to whinnying.

Across the valley where the trail we were to follow came out of the forest I saw a single pack horse running alone. Sensing his fellows on the opposite height he stopped instantly and sent a whinnying cry across to them. They eagerly answered. Creatures enslaved, calling in their loneliness to one another across a valley, across space, across time. Pierced by a sudden perception of the agony of all creation, I almost wept, watching with my Indian pony a long line of other horses come into sight packed high with burdens and heading for heartbreaking heights, that men might have food and shelter. From the reaches of my being there flooded back upon my heart the groanings and travailings of life that cannot be uttered.

At two o'clock, with raindrops falling, the crowd of us mounted, rode down to the creek, crossed it and then took the trail on the opposite side of the valley where a sign read: To Og Pass.

The ride to Og Pass, after lunch, soon brought us to a succession of narrow ledges upon which we rode around the shoulders of mountains burned bare of forest years ago, many blackened trees still standing in the midst of desolation. On our sixty horses went, putting one foot in front of another until, at the end of what seemed ages to me, we wound through narrow Og Pass into a wide green land, hemmed on the left with mountains at whose feet a stream flowed. This looked like Paradise after what we had come through.

Here our horses visibly rejoiced, trotting in spite of us, or stopping, in spite of us, to crop the luscious verdure. When Scottie was having a bite I turned in my saddle and, looking back, saw a glorious sight, the meeting of the mountains through which we had come, deep blue now in the distance.

The flowers were particularly lovely from Brewster Ranger's Cabin to Og Pass, and again in this sun-brighted plain. Alpine forget-me-nots of intensest blue, set off by proximity to the pale yellow mountain honeysuckle, the lilac coloured rough fleabane, the bright yellow of shrubby cinqfoil, and the white blossoms of birch-leaved spiræa. There were many flowers I cannot name.

After a few moments' rest, our cavalcade rode on through wide green stretches at the foot of heights that towered on our left, until, suddenly rounding a turn, the peak of Mount Assiniboine was revealed to us, looking extraordinarily like the Matterhorn.

Small lakes marked our way. As the afternoon advanced there were views all about us of peaks rising into the clear blue sky. I rode the twentieth in the line, enjoying as often today sight of the riders—dark moving objects—far ahead, establishing what an artist calls "scale" in the surrounding picture of immensities.

Finally the trail led into a stretch of shrub growth and buffalo bush to the horses' knees. We came out of it on a fine level plateau on the north side of Mount Assiniboine.

5:30 P. M. Saturday afternoon. On Assiniboine Plateau:—While the indefatigable camp workers and guides are hurrying to get tepees up and duffle distributed, the Trail Riders stand about in groups, or do as I am doing, recline thankfully against a pile of duffle. How blessed this green vale looks to me, with its peaceful sunlight, and horses at rest even if mere man has to work. Over the heads of the creatures, I see at the end of the long plateau the majestic, snowy pyramid of Mount Assiniboine lifting itself 11,820 feet into a cloudless blue heaven. As I gaze, my thought runs back mile by mile along the trail travelled today and yesterday—from here to Og Pass, to Brewster Creek Cabin, to Banff. In rain and sunshine we have ridden through bog land and forest, beside lakes and streams, over burned mountains and stony ledges, to a green and smiling plateau. We have reached our destination, and here we are to rest for two nights and a whole day. Blissful prospect!

The altitude here is 7,500 feet. The lessened oxygen content in the air makes one feel lazy, and it will be best not to do much at first. But tomorrow I would like to explore the surrounding area for flowers. Dan no doubt will be happy holding a rod over Marvel Lake, which is not far away.

Sunday, August 1. Written at various times:—Dinner last night, at six P. M., was a genuine one, ranging from soup to roast lamb with vegetables and condiments, and on to fruit and coffee. (All canned goods, salt and smoked meats were "packed in" two days ago and stored in the cook's tent.) I asked about bears and was told there are not many around now. But I should think even one were enough to eat up supplies.

After dinner a big fire was built, and around it, at a comfortable distance, logs were placed, upon which everyone sat, or against which they leaned. A portable little organ was brought out and Mr. Allen Crawford, an excellent musician, played accompaniments for a sing-song, Mr. John Murray Gibbon directing.

A young man with a guitar, whom we had heard at Kananaskis, sang ranch songs to his own accompaniment.

The program finished, cocoa was served and we all scattered to quarters, looking forward with eagerness to all we should do and see tomorrow.

The two pretty sisters from Lethbridge, Leola and Mona Watson, Miss Ida Sandman and I were no sooner in our tepee preparing for the night's sleep than we heard the sound of rain drops falling on the tight canvas around us. Alas!

On Sunday morning, August first, I awoke before five o'clock. While the others slept I lay watching snow-flakes drift down through the open top into the circle of the fireplace a few inches from the side of my sleeping-bag. I sat up and reached for a cup of water I had spent fifteen minutes in getting at the brook, last night; the water had become ice, and the cup itself was surrounded with snow where I had set it in the open, outside the edge of the tepee. Jingo, it was cold! Snow at Mount Assiniboine on the first day of August. Here was ad-venture!

CHAPTER XVIII

ALONE ON THE GREAT DIVIDE

When the sing-song ended our first evening at Assiniboine, it didn't take me long to crawl into my little
white pup tent (the same I'd used at Brewster's Creek).
Taking off my boots, I got into the eider-down sleeping-
bag just as I was. This Trail Ride was giving me my
first experience with eider-down; that bag seemed like
heaven. For a moment I lay thinking of the fun the fishermen of this party were going to have in the morning,
at Marvel Lake; in fact I was landing a ten-pound trout
when I fell sound asleep.

I awoke feeling refreshed, at the same time noticing
that the top and sides of the tent were sagging till in
places they touched my blankets. My watch showed six-
thirty A. M. Time to get up. I rolled over, reached for the
tent flap, and poked my head out—into deep snow! And
snow was falling thick and fast! Very much as a turtle
would have done, I drew in my head, laughing. It was
all so darned funny; people in the East suffering with
heat waves and we in the West enjoying on the first day
of August what looked very much like a blizzard. Com-

pletely forgetting that the snow had stopped all ventilation in my small enclosure, I lighted a cigarette, reached for my boots and put them on. But before I could get the boots laced I had to rush out into the open for air.

It was a queer, ghostlike world that I saw. Except the cooks, who were busy about their fires, there was no one to be seen. The great mass of Assiniboine that we had looked upon last evening was gone; now there was nothing to be seen but very white tents sticking up from a whiter plateau. I was seized with a wild desire to run to the whitened tepees and shout "Merry Christmas," but the smell of bacon frying hurried me over to the grub tent. I had never felt so hungry.

Chester, a guide of Kananaskis Ranch, and an Indian helper named Paul, from Morley Reservation, had just come in from a night in the mountains, and as we four ate breakfast he told me a story that made an eiderdown sleeping-bag look like the Waldorf-Astoria.

The hundred and twenty horses that brought men, women, and provisions into the Assiniboine Plateau yesterday afternoon had to be taken to ground where they could feed during the night. This night riding was Chester's job and, in company with Paul the Indian, he set out with the horses after an early supper.

"Gosh what a night!" exclaimed Chester as we tucked way the bacon. "About midnight Paul and I lighted a fire on top of a ridge, to keep warm. A little later it

[157]

began to snow, and soon I couldn't hear the horses' bells. I went off to round them up, leaving Paul to keep the fire burning. You remember Og Pass that we rode through early yesterday afternoon?"

"Certainly do," I replied, "and the green our horses stopped to eat."

"Well, they must have remembered the grass," said Chester. "I had to ride almost to Og Pass before I caught up with them. By the time I had rounded the horses up and started back for the ridge it was snowing so hard I couldn't see a darn thing. Half the time I didn't know where I was, what with the darkness and the snow in my eyes. But I must have been going in the right direction, because after riding for hours I saw high up ahead of me what I knew was the gleam of our fire. Believe me I was glad to see it. Paul and I stayed right there with the horses till dawn came, then started back. And here I am." Turning to the cook Chester called, "Give us another cup of coffee, and after that I'm going to the tent, and will I sleep!"

The Duchess and her three companions must be awake, I thought, and, wondering a bit how they were getting on, I gathered an armful of short wood and walked to their tepee.

"Anybody up?" I called.

"Hurrah, come on in." I pushed aside the flap of canvas and crawled into the tepee. Four heads were sticking out of the ends of what might have been four big brown cocoons.

"What does the thermometer say?" asked little Leola Watson of Lethbridge, Alberta.

"Feels like about twenty above," I answered, as I set a match to dry kindling and saw a flame catch three pyramided sticks of wood.

"There you are," I said to them. "You can warm your boots. And hurry, breakfast is now being served in the dining-car, and believe me it's good." With that I made my way out.

Many Trail Riders were moving about in the white scene; the darkness of these figures against the snow, now about four inches deep, made me think of Eskimo pictures of the Arctic that Robert Flaherty once gave me.

Carl Rungius began making snow sculpture and produced the likeness of a dog that almost wagged its tail. Then Dan McCowan and I made a snow man that started a competition. Meanwhile, where the sing-song had been last night, a huge fire was burning.

Our Sunday newspaper that day was a matter of verbal contributions to what might be called a Society Page and a Personal Column. One of the items I remember told of sleeping-bags which, their tags having been lost, got into wrong hands. A lady discovered, too late to do anything about it, that the pyjamas she drew out from the bottom of her bag were designed to fit a large male; and she wondered what that large male managed to do with the small suit that she had likewise left in the bottom of her bag for safe keeping.

While all of us were amusing ourselves one way and another, the guides and camp workers rode horses into the nearby forest and hauled out by a rope attached to their saddles great tree trunks which were sawed and split for the insatiable fires of the cook tents and the tepees. The Duchess caught sight of her Scottie hauling a log down to the camp and, when he was released from his job, went to pay him a visit. She came back and said it was very disillusioning to find that, after all they had gone through together, Scottie's response to her greeting was a look that indicated he really wasn't interested.

In the afternoon a group of us decided it would be fun to walk to Lake Magog and have tea at the Mount Assiniboine Camp owned and run by the ski professional of Lake Placid Club, whom many knew well, Erling Strom. With the snow still falling we set out on the three-mile hike. It was heavy going, but good tea beside a fire in a pleasant room set us up for the return trip.

Many who knew well the mountain area in which we were that week-end agreed they had never seen so heavy a fall of snow at that particular time of year. When I told this to the Duchess she replied: "Well, you remember don't you, Dan, that the winter we spent in Florence the river Arno for the first time in thirty years froze solid from bank to bank? We're lucky; Mother Nature always puts on a good show when she hears we're coming."

It snowed at Assiniboine Plateau until Monday morning. About ten o'clock, all the horses having been saddled, and all the duffle packed, the Trail Riders started out, making their way through a blank white cover that had been laid over the land.

Through Rock Pass and down into the Valley of the Rocks we rode. This was no sooner accomplished than we found ourselves with magical suddenness in a world filled with sunshine. The effect couldn't have been more astonishing if a New Year's Day should bloom into Fourth of July.

It was a happy crowd that rode the trail down into small Golden Valley, and that there followed Porcupine Creek to levels near a ranger's cabin. Once there, everyone dismounted to rest in the warm sunlight while eating lunch.

Facing us as we reclined on the good green earth was the terrific ascent of Porcupine Mountain, high upon which, even then, part of the pack train of horses was zigzagging its way across bare brown earth and rocks, to the wooded heights of Citadel Pass. A half hour later we followed the pack horses up Porcupine.

It was on the steepest part of the ascent to Citadel Pass that my "charger" gave out completely. While at the ranch it had been hard to hold him in, even with a curbed bit, since we'd been in the mountains he had grown milder and milder, until most of the time I had found myself at the end of the line of riders instead of at the head. Now when the altitude was nearing 8,000 feet, the thoroughbred half of my horse gave out and I was left with the other half, holding up the line. A guide came by, trying to find the trouble, took one look at my handsome bay and said:

"He's done for. We'll have to turn him loose; it's the altitude. I'll give you a pack horse." So pots and pans were taken off Sandy and my saddle replaced his load.

"Has Sandy any tricks?" I asked as I mounted him.

"He may want to go to sleep," Chester answered, laughing. "Better get a switch." While this scene was taking place the riders I had held back were passing, and as they went by they razzed me with:

"Too bad, Dan, that you killed your horse" or "It's thoughtful of you, Dan, to provide beef for dinner." Meanwhile my former mount was obviously having a good time, eating everything green in sight.

"Perhaps it was all a bluff," I thought, as I started old Sandy along the trail, "and the swanky bay is having a laugh at my expense."

By this time the entire cavalcade had disappeared over

the rise ahead. Sandy and I were alone.

Sandy had my number before we had more than started, and he stopped to eat whenever he liked. The switch was brought into play, so, between eating and beating, Sandy and I came into a great plateau on the top of the world. We were absolutely alone, not a horse nor a rider could be seen; all were lost to sight in some fold of the Great Divide.

Sandy didn't like being alone. He stopped and whinnied. I beat him, but he wouldn't move. He threw up his head and whinnied again, then seemed to listen. I listened too, and, from far down the valley that Sandy and I had just come up, a faint tinkle of bells was on the air —the pack train with some of Sandy's friends. He was for going back; I was for going forward. I talked to him, told him there were other horses just ahead. He lowered his nose to the ground and sniffed, then raised his head and listened, smelled of the earth again, and came to the decision that the horses ahead were nearer than the horses behind us. Upon that, he ambled off in the direction I had been trying to persuade him to take.

Speed? Sandy would have none of it. Where there were good things to eat he stopped and took his fill. My switch by now was reduced to practically nothing, and some of the hair on Sandy's rear end had grown thin. Then I came to a conclusion and lighted my pipe. Even if Sandy decided to lie down and take a nap, the pack

[163]

train would pick me up. I gave myself to the strange sensation of being alone on the top of the world.

Toward evening, Sandy and I strolled down a wide green slope and on past Sunshine Lodge. The pack train, after all, had gone by us without our knowing, because here were the tents and tepees already set up in a rich green vale near the ranger's cabin. Fires were burning, smoke rising into the clear air.

A distracted Duchess rushed to greet me, exclaiming, "Where in the world have you two been?"

"You two!" Sandy's personality had at once impressed itself upon the Duchess, even as it had impressed itself upon me all the afternoon.

The big lounge of Sunshine Ski Lodge (15 miles southwest of Banff on the Continental Divide, at Timber Line) was crowded to capacity with Trail Riders the evening of the day we left Assiniboine Plateau. As the Duchess and I sat with all the others in the warm and attractive room, laughing and talking under bright lights, the tepee fires of Assiniboine seemed a long way off.

At the invitation of Mr. and Mrs. Pat Brewster, we were gathered under the roof at Sunshine Lodge for our evening sing-song, and this one was held especially to arrange a program for the final big Pow Wow at Sundance Canyon the following night.

Mount Assiniboine

John Murray Gibbon, always a moving spirit in events, together with R. H. Palenske, called on this one and that one until a program was built up. Mrs. Pat Brewster's songs, Jean Hembroff's recitations, Colonel Moore's stories, Allen Crawford's accordion playing, the Duchess's poem about forest rangers filled an hour with fun and laughter. Hot cocoa sent everyone to their beds feeling that the world was a good place and trail riding its finest fun.

CHAPTER XIX

END OF THE BIG RIDE

The Duchess's Diary

I SHALL always remember the last sunny morning of the Trail Ride—at breakfast time the tables set out under a cloudless sky, and all the jolly crowd circling round, gathering what they wished to eat, and then, each one with his plate, finding a seat near a big fire of flaming logs; for remember, at 7,800 feet altitude the wind coming down from Simpson Pass wasn't exactly a Florida zephyr.

A sense of ease took possession of us; we were not to start the ride back to Banff until one o'clock. Whole hours could be loafed away sitting within the circle of warmth, looking down into the rich green glade where our encampment had been, watching the guides stripping canvas from tepee poles and packing it on horses that stood quietly awaiting their loads.

The sunlight had a knife-edge brightness. Wrapped in Mrs. Rungius's blanket coat I watched the fuzzy seed heads of the Western anemone swing in the breeze, for-

[166]

getting self in the beauty of earth and sky that surrounded us, glad there was time for the beauty to sink
into the texture of one's being.

After I had sewed up a tear in Carl Rungius's
breeches, he and Dan found them a nice rock, and then,
sitting back to back supporting each other, basked in
the sunlight. The silent man in the narrow-brimmed felt
hat, who, like one of Chaucer's pilgrims, has so often
ridden alone these days, stood looking on at the group
beside the fire. He is shy. I made him talk the other day
and found him a pleasant person.

The officers of the Trail Riders Association rode out
of camp an hour after the pack train left and an hour
before the rest of us, because they had to make arrangements and hold a meeting before the big Pow Wow in
Sundance Canyon brings the 1937 Trail Ride to an end.

During the early luncheon while I listened with the
first part of my mind to fine Mr. Sibbald tell about his
father, a missionary (of great accomplishment) to the
Stony Indians, the second part of my mind was saying
with mingled regret and anticipation: "There is only
Healy Creek between us and Banff, Banff where golf is
played, and tea is served on club porches and orchestras
dispense sweet music. It is impossible," ran the murmur-
ing in my mind, "that there should be any more such
hair-raising situations for man and beast as we have gone
through since last Friday."

Away from the green glade near Simpson Pass rode our whole company down a steep descent of outcropping rock; and from that moment, the trail I had thought of with complacency went terribly down; in fact, to me, the decline and fall of the Roman Empire seemed, by comparison, a colourless incident. I'll say nothing of the next hour and a half; the fact that we were among forest trees helped to divert my thoughts.

How beautiful seemed the woodland level where we found Healy Creek running; all too soon we were out in the open, and then our horses began to climb.

Where was Dan? I had been asking myself, all the afternoon, and when, a little after four o'clock, we reached the pine grove in Sundance Canyon where the Trail Ride ended, he was still nowhere to be seen. One by one we gave up the horses that had so faithfully served us; their saddles were stripped off, and they were led to the corral. It wasn't till an hour later, when I was about to send out a search party, that Dan came in, whistling. He'd broken a stirrup strap, and this, together with a few other incidents, had given him the kind of time he enjoys.

Now motors drove up from Banff bringing interesting people from all around. By the time the program was to begin the big marquee tent was crowded. There were speeches by important persons, and lovely songs by a professional singer. Our part of the program went smoothly, thanks to the rehearsal at Sunshine Lodge.

It was a happy and enthusiastic lot of Trail Riders that at the hour's end went out together, under the starry sky to where motors were waiting to carry them back to Banff.

FOREST RANGERS

Forest Rangers riding to the High Sierras,
Sixteen pack mules, their packs looming white,
Splash across the creek to the trail that leads upward,
Grey dawn edging the black rim of night:

Dew along the stream-bottom, sharp tang of sage,
Creaking of leather, jingling of spurs,
Muffled pad of climbing feet, sharpened by a ringing—
Steel striking stone where the patient feet strain
Up and up. Now the winds begin sighing
Five thousand up, where the pinion pine grows. . . .
Sudden, comes a glory! The red sun pouring
Like a prairie fire over distant desert hills.
Higher up, and higher now, the narrow trail clinging
To sheer granite face. . . . Through the morning it
    winds.
Off to the east, see, the desert ranges rising;
Argus, and the Panamints old smoky Slate:
Bordering Death Valley where bones lie bleaching
Silent in the sands of a thousand thousand years.

[169]

Eleven o'clock! Through the gap called Farewell.
A last look down at the world far below. . . .
Then, westward again, with a cold wind blowing
Fresh from high fields that are glittering with snow.

Noon. One o'clock. Whoa! The hungry mules are
　　halted,
Fed, and the stiff-legged men are glad to walk.
Hands are warmed at a fire where a gallon pot is boil-
　　ing;
Sam throws into it a fist full of tea.
Then each man eats what his saddle-bag provides him.
Stamping, and stretching, the train's on its way.
Fighting now through snow-drifts on wind-swept
　　ledges,
Plunging into swollen streams of water, cold as ice.
The patient mules are lagging, men hunching in their
　　saddles.
It's a long day since dawn and a long time since noon.
Finally toward sunset shines a fenced green meadow
Near a log cabin. Ho! Shelter for the night!
The trail's end is reached. Men fling themselves from
　　horses,
Strip the heavy packs from the backs of weary mules.
There's fire, and food. Then, rest after straining,
While smoke rises upward to meet the coming dark.

Snowdrifts of memory melt in the firelight,
Muscles relax, tired eyelids close.
Two gallant men, with sixteen pack mules,
Guarding mighty forests from fire and foes.

CHAPTER XX

MOTORING TO LAKE MORAINE

The Duchess's Diary

Written at Larch Valley Camp, Sunday afternoon, August 8:—Between the evening of August third, when we returned to Banff Springs Hotel from the Trail Ride to Mount Assiniboine, and the morning of August fifth, Dan and I did nothing, in a dozen different ways, and with great delight. After breakfast on the fifth I had to attack the job of repacking those sixteen pieces of luggage with which we had so light-heartedly departed from Montreal five weeks earlier. Trying to foresee what clothing we should need in a variety of unknown circumstances, I set about packing bags to be left in storage in Banff, bags to be sent ahead to Vancouver, and bags to accompany us on the Trail Hike beginning at Lake Moraine the following day. Just when I had become convinced that I couldn't possibly finish in time to get a train to Lake Louise, we received an invitation from Mr. John Murray Gibbon, the distinguished Canadian writer and poet, to drive with him at three o'clock to that gathering place for the hikers to Larch Valley.

It was with infinite relief and pleasure that I sank into a seat in Mr. Gibbon's motor at the appointed hour. My work was done; we would be out of doors all the afternoon; there would be an opportunity to talk with a man whose accomplishments I greatly admired; and we were going to a place I loved. It wasn't until our car was passing the Beaver Dams, on Vermilion Lake, that I suddenly realized I had had no lunch.

Many delicate-leaved aspens, trembling in the soft air, shook sunlight in golden showers beside our way, while off to the left, across a valley, dark pointed pines on purple-shadowed mountains brooded in the afternoon light.

Suddenly to the right, high on a cliff beside the road, a Rocky Mountain sheep appeared, head, with beautifully curved horns, held high as he stood motionless. Then six little sheep, on slender legs, came jumping into the scene, and stopped on the instant, holding their heads erect with awareness. Our car was drawn up to the side of the road, that we might watch for a moment these wild creatures that were looking upon us, unafraid. A car coming from the opposite direction slowed down; everyone in it, like ourselves, smiled at the charming sight. As suddenly as they had come, the sheep, with trigger-like swiftness, started away into the forest.

Light effects on the towering Sawback Range to the southwest grew to magnificence as four o'clock drew on; mountain flanks deep in shadow would be seen juxtaposed against others full in the sunlight, the rich green of their forests running nearly to peaks that cut the blue immensity of the sky.

When we reached Johnson Canyon Mr. Gibbon told the chauffeur that we would stop at the restaurant for tea. At sound of the word "tea" the sinking feeling in my insides, due to no food for seven hours, was changed to a feeling of serenity; and twenty minutes later it was a much refreshed me who with the others got back into the car. I had not only enjoyed food and drink, but, along with Mr. Gibbon, Mr. Palenske, and Dan, had laughed heartily. The proprietor of the Johnson Canyon establishment told us some exceedingly funny stories, one after the other, and so fast that the details, as I laughed, got blurred and ran into one another. Now, eight hours afterward, his story of a bear and neat little King Prajodapok of Siam (who left behind him in the Canadian Rockies an indelible impression) has got mixed with another about a lady and a glacier; and if I should try to tell either of them here, I'm sure I would put the bear on the ice, and send the king and the lady trail riding together, which would never do.

The car bore us on again, through sunlight. As Mr. Gibbon and I conversed, I learned that the road we were travelling had been built by interned Austrians during the Great War (Austrians, where are you now?); and I heard about a new trail to Consolation Lakes, blazed, some years ago, by Mr. Gibbon and Mr. James Brewster, proprietor of Sunshine Lodge near Simpson Pass, familiarly known as "Jim"; and that the founder of the Alpine Club of Canada, Mr. A. O. Wheeler—A.C.; F.R.G.S.—whom I should meet at the end of the Trail Hike, had made many fine maps of the mountain area for the Canadian Government.

About five o'clock a turn in the ascending road brought a sweeping sight of purple mountains with the light of the sun behind them; Mount Pilot, the inevitable, far to the south; and nearer, toward the west, majestic Mount Temple, a white mantle of glacial snow and ice about its shoulders, rose into view as our way ascended.

We drifted to talk of books, I congratulating Mr. Gibbon on his splendid achievement in writing *Steel of Empire*, a story of the building of the Canadian Pacific Railway which is at the same time a history of the development of the West. It wasn't long before we had got to the rock bottom of literature—and (to me) of life—poetry. My companion delighted me by remarking that much so-called poetry written today is a by-product of the cross-word puzzle. At that moment our car swept past the road to Moraine Lake which we hikers will be taking tomorrow. The next thing I knew we were within the grounds of the Chateau Lake Louise; the lake's blue waters and snowy guardian peaks were spread before our eyes, and we were being welcomed by the manager of the Chateau, Mr. J. J. Meredith. Dan and I were soon established in a room overlooking the lake. It was like coming home.

Miss Elizabeth Booz of Washington, Pa., an honourary member of the Sky Line Trail Hikers, was present at a jolly dinner given by Mr. Gibbon. Afterward we all went out to walk upon the terrace, amid the evening loveliness of Lake Louise.

A voice, singing in the hotel's wide promenade, drew us indoors. When the program of songs ended we were lured into the ball-room by music of an orchestra, where, seated in deep chairs, we watched the assembled guests.

Suddenly Eugene Kaufmann, a fellow trail rider from Philadelphia, hove to in front of me and suggested that we show the crowd how to dance. He was shod in rubber-soled shoes, as I was. (All my evening clothes had been sent to Vancouver.)

"Oh, come on," he urged; "let's show them the Gutta Percha Hop." I couldn't resist, and we went onto the floor for a waltz that was great fun in spite of its lack of glide. "Gene" was in a somewhat elated frame of mind, I discovered, and put on flourishes that amused the crowd.

When, at ten o'clock the next morning, a bus with open sides arrived at the Chateau to take us to the starting point of the hike, its top was up against rain that came slanting down out of a grey sky. With plenty of warm things under raincoats, Miss Booz, Miss Harper and I got into the bus. Three big men—Mr. Gibbon, Mr. Palenske, and Dan—took the seat behind the driver to make a wind-break for us.

We drove off, stopping in a moment or two at Deer Lodge, where we picked up Mr. Allen Crawford, dispenser of music, who was carrying the priceless organ that has gone over mountain passes on the backs of horses with trail hikers and trail riders for many a year.

Now we took the road to Lake Moraine, wide and well-built, which, after a short descent, rose steadily. In spite of the greyness there were magnificent views of distant ranging mountains. We experienced breathtaking moments as our car followed the curving, clinging road built years ago. Going steadily on we found ourselves looking down into deep, winding valleys through drifting mist and occasional showers. I grew to love grey misty weather when living in Paris, and this ride of three quarters of an hour was for me filled with beauty.

In forty-five minutes our motor reached the shore of Moraine Lake and parked near the Lodge and bungalows which stand in a forest clearing. We hurried indoors where a friendly greeting awaited us and a big open fire. Putting aside raincoats we all gathered near the warmth and glow of burning logs. Sitting there snug and dry I was filled with a delightful sense of security, which a sudden downpour of rain on the roof heightened.

The door of the Lodge opened and in from the pouring rain came a group of eight to join us; chairs were moved back, and they were taken into the fireside circle. Being absolutely green at this kind of thing, I was greatly puzzled at the prospect. Would our leader really set forth up the mountain in such weather, I wondered, when all one could hope for at the end of the hike was a wet tepee? Looking about upon the dozen attractive persons, I almost burst out laughing as in my mind I saw them coming from afar out of comfortable homes, to hike in the rain. (But I laughed too soon.)

Some of the late comers went to the prettily set tables and tucked away tea and a snack. They had sense, I thought to myself, sense that probably was born of experience, and I found myself wishing that Dan and I had done the same thing.

All at once I saw Mr. Gibbon putting on his raincoat. That was the signal; everyone followed his example. Then, picking up our alpenstocks, one after the other we went bravely out into the falling rain.

CHAPTER XXI

TRAIL HIKE

FROM Moraine Lake the trail to Larch Valley led at first through forest, and it was the trees that gave me heart, the sweet breath of their branches lifted my spirits; then the enchanting little streams we crossed made the rain-drops falling from the sky seem an artistic touch on the part of Nature. A sense of release, of freedom, increased within me as we walked steadily up and onward, wood-land flowers glistening in wet loveliness along the way.

The altitude is 6,200 feet at Moraine Lake, where we started. When we had climbed for half an hour, the trail, out of the forest now, grew steeper, and the line would occasionally halt. Mrs. A. O. Wheeler, wife of the distinguished explorer, followed our leader, Mr. Gibbon. After her, and immediately in front of me, came Mr. Dan McCowan, the naturalist, with his camera, and his charming wife. Behind me, the official doctor of the Trail Hike, Robert Gow, M.D., was followed by my Dan, and below him there were, I knew, twenty others I couldn't see, who made up the number come from all over to spend three days at a central camp in Larch Valley from which they could go out on further hikes.

Lake Moraine, below us, seen from a constantly increasing height, grew more and more intensely blue. I was gazing at this sight when the sun emerged from the clouds, and at once the temperature rose.

About two thirds of the way to the top I suddenly became dizzy and weak, and the air passages in my head seemed to have closed. Dr. Gow said: "Off with your raincoat, and your leather coat—they keep the body from breathing." After sitting for a moment I recovered and went along without more trouble, but I shall always remember with amusement the miraculous refreshment brought about by a peppermint lozenge bestowed upon me by Dan McCowan.

(Portrait: of the Duchess and a peppermint lozenge!)

When everyone on the trail, above me and below, had divested himself of his raincoat, clouds shut out the sun and rain began to fall again.

At two-ten P. M. after what seemed to me a marvellously steep climb, we were near the top, when suddenly I smelled, through the misty dampness, wood smoke. "Oh blessed scent!" I said to myself. "The camp is not far off."

At a crossing of trails Mr. Gibbon turned right, taking the one marked: "To Sentinel Pass." We plodded along. All at once ahead of us two figures appeared in the way, and I heard someone exclaim, "It's Mr. and

Fay Glacier and Moraine Lake

Mrs. Whyte, our president and his wife." This reception committee guided us into Larch Valley at about two-forty-five P. M.

Sight of the Indian tepees, set in a green lowland of blazing fires, and cooks on the jump around a long canvas-roofed table loaded with things to eat, warmed me to the heart. In a second the crowd of us were seated around that table, and when my eye lighted on a big bowl of salad and dishes of vegetables, I knew that I was in for a good time. There was beef, there was hot coffee. In no time at all the world became marvellous, and Larch Valley the best place in it.

A train of pack horses came into Larch Valley encampment about three-thirty, while we were finishing our dinner. They had climbed the same trail, loaded, in half the time it had taken us, travelling light—which made me feel pretty small. Now, the guide rapidly unpacked each horse, stacking the duffle where we all could get it; then, mounting his own horse, he rounded up the others and, driving them before him, was soon out of sight, bound for the bottom again to bring up the fourth and last load of the day.

By this time mists were retreating from the lower slopes of Mount Temple, close on the east. From a western slope a stand of lovely Lyall larches became visible, and we saw stretching before us the floor of Larch Valley thickly carpeted with shrub growth and patterned

[181]

with a narrow silver stream that came winding down out of the north.

Among the brown tents and white tepees camp helpers and guides were moving busily, carrying duffle here and there, or wood for the morning and the evening fires. The thirty-odd hikers themselves, refreshed by a good dinner, took on the business of arranging their quarters for the three-day stay.

Dan found he was to be with Mr. Gibbon, Mr. Palenske, and his artist friend Carl Rungius, in the big white chief's tepee, the only one decorated with Indian designs. I was to share a large tepee with Mrs. A. O. Wheeler, to whom I already felt attracted, and Mrs. James Simpson, a delightful person who was the president-elect of the Sky Line Trail Hikers.

The business of getting settled went something like this: you ran to the storage tepee and, grabbing a cotton mattress from the pile, lugged it to your own tepee. After a conference with your companions, you chose a section of the ground enclosed by the canvas walls. Upon that ground, now yours by right of eminent domain, you laid down your mattress (to keep off dampness), and on it spread your sleeping-bag. Quite simple? Not at all. Though you could have made, when at home, as good a bed as a hospital nurse, that knowledge would have done little for you in Larch Valley. There, if you wanted your head higher than your heels, it was neces-

sary to adjust yourself to circumstances, always a delicate matter, requiring nicety and intelligence. Lacking
these qualities, I threw myself down on the mattress to
learn in the doing, as recommended by the devotees of
Progressive Education. The results were not too satisfactory, but I decided to let it go at that, and saying,
"So much for earth, now for the heavens," I cast an eye
upward to that strange aperture at the top of a tepee
especially arranged to let out the smoke of a fire burning directly below it.

Would rain and snow come in as easily as smoke would
go out? Yes, the evidence was on the ground—a circle
wet by the late showers. Taking a stick I drew a line
around the circle's circumference, and then adjusted my
mattress so there was a margin of three inches between
it and the fire line.

There still remains to be mentioned the matter of the
door. Of course, in the ordinary sense of the word, a
tepee has no door. By bending, one gets in and out
through a low aperture, afterward closing it to wind,
storm, and visitors by a loose piece of canvas—and when
I say loose I mean loose—which is always outside, either
on the ground, or thrown back upon the sloping side
of the tepee itself. The skill expended in making Indian
bead-work is nothing compared with that required to
keep this loose piece of canvas in place across the exit,
when wind is blowing. After one has worked feverishly

and finally succeeded in making the thing stay "put," one is sure to be smitten with a desire to go down to the brook for a drink of water.

The amazing thing is that one becomes enamoured of tepees; they are astonishingly comfortable, far more so than tents, because in them one can have a fire.

If you happened to have brought a piece of string in your pocket, you fastened an end of it to one of the eight supporting poles of the tepee, and another end to another pole, and *Voilà!* a line upon which to hang a wet stocking, or a necktie. You were in residence!

The first night, after having got carefully and comfortably tucked into your sleeping-bag, you discovered that everything you wanted at hand was just beyond reach. This taught you to always have your duffle bag (a little one!) close to your head. You learned it was best when you took off your boots (almost all there was to getting to bed) to keep them beside you under the edge of your sleeping-bag so they wouldn't be any colder in the morning; and you kept within the sleeping-bag every article of clothing, because during the nights dew wets the canvas sides of the tepee and falls through its top opening. Anything left around during the night is too wet for comfort the next morning until dried by the sun or the heat of a fire, both of which may or may not be present.

The historic first night in a tepee, if you are a new

hand at camping, you exclaim, "Why did I come!" The last night of a camping trip you say to somebody you have learned to like tremendously—because only the very nicest people love the out-of-doors, "How can I possibly leave?" But to get back:

Between four and seven o'clock of August sixth, there were showers and an occasional effort at clearing; then, toward eight o'clock, wide rifts in the clouds above the towering Ten Peaks revealed breath-taking glory. But before sunset the pack train came in again, with the last of the duffle. After the loads had been removed, rack, blanket, and bridle were stripped from each horse, a flat bell hung on a leather strap was fastened closed on each horse's neck, and with a pat on the rump one after the other the patient beasts were turned loose just as they were, all hot and hungry, into the cool of the coming night. The wild horse expects to gather his own food and drink, but this seemed short rations to me; yet, as far as one could see, the horses were in good condition.

With assurance in the sky of a clear evening, the men lighted a fire of great logs around which other logs were drawn to provide seats, and the whole crowd drew together around the glowing warmth. Allen Crawford warmed our spirits with the music of his accordion, and then played accompaniments to songs of the Trail which everyone sang, until darkness and a round of hot cocoa sent us to our quarters for the night.

I awoke before five o'clock; my companions along the opposite side of the tepee were lost to sight under piled blankets. Warm and comfortable in my sleeping-bag I lay waiting for the time when I might get up, watching, through the opening above me, a bit of sky enchantingly blue.

At six o'clock I sat up and found the temperature cold! After tidying myself—it couldn't be called dressing—I slipped out of the bag and proceeded to get into my boots, *the* boots which had brought me here all the way from Connecticut. Stiff and cold they were. I watched my sleeping partners because what I wanted, intensely, was to get out into the stillness of morning without talking; to experience the full impact of the mountains at early morning, alone.

Very quietly I moved aside the canvas that covered the tepee's entrance—looking back at the sleepers I saw they had not been disturbed—slipped quickly through the opening, replaced the canvas, and, instinctively throwing my head back to draw in a long breath of the cold, aromatic air, I looked up.

High above the highest peaks surrounding me where I stood, alone, arched a completely cloudless heaven. Ethereal blue eastward above Mount Temple, and clear to the south where far below I knew Moraine Lake was lying; on to the west, over Fay, and Little, Deltaform and all the Ten Peaks, yes, sweeping north to Pinnacle

Mountain and Sentinel Pass until it came, full circle, to Temple again—blue sky!

A golden radiance filled Larch Valley, mingling with an atmosphere of tonic freshness as it poured over eastern heights that as yet hid the orb of the sun. Surrounded by a stillness as tremendous as the mountains themselves, and a light of piercing loveliness, I moved slowly to a rise of land south of the encampment; there I turned to face the way I had come and saw stretching before me the whole silvered valley.

From the valley's far-away northern end, where Pinnacle Mountain rose to the sky, there came to me the whiteness of water falling without any sound to frosted levels, and the gleam of water winding through growth of a grey-green bottom, until it flowed into the open near white canvas tepees whose sloping sides rose shining with frozen dew.

Close to me where I was sitting, frost glistened on green leaf, on grey rock, on the white immaculate bloom of everlasting that my hand touched as I prayed to be given ten minutes now for joy of the spirit within me.

Amidst silence encircled by silver enchantment I held myself as still as once upon a time did Criseyde.

CHAPTER XXII

LARCH VALLEY

The Duchess's Diary

As THE golden orb of the sun rose above the rocky eastern rim, a guide came out of a big brown tent far down at the other end of the encampment—first man on the scene. He was quickly followed by another. Nearer me a movement at the three-foot entrance of the Big Chief's tepee attracted my attention, and I suddenly saw Dan, with a writhing of his six-foot-six frame, wiggle out into the open, stand up, and glance about. He began walking in my direction and when near enough exclaimed with a wide gesture:

"Look at it! Would you take it for the same place we came into yesterday?" Sitting down beside me he gazed upon the scene.

For a few minutes longer the valley was ours, and then, all at once, the whole encampment awoke. Men and women, young and older, came piling out of tepees into the shining sunlight. Some ran to the brook to wash their faces (below the point where drinking water was obtained), others filled basins at the brook, then, setting up housekeeping on a log, went at the business of shaving. Young girls combed their pretty hair and laughed with one another for the sheer joy of living.

As a smell of frying bacon came to us on the faintly stirring air, Dan and I watched the activities around the cook tent with increasing interest.

"Gosh, Duchess! my mouth is watering," exclaimed Dan. A moment later Bert, the cook (whose dinner and supper the day before had proved he knew his business) sounded the gong for breakfast. We were up in an instant and raced down to the long table set under an awning, taking places on the inside, that we might look out upon the Ten Peaks. Fruit, oatmeal porridge, bacon, ham, eggs, toast, pancakes, coffee—gallons of it—and fun! Everybody laughing and joking with those beside him or across the table.

Each morning after breakfast at a cleared place in the open centre of the encampment, a great log fire is built and lighted, to be put out only when the last person goes to bed at night. This fire is the heart of the hiker's adventure, drawing to itself, throughout the waking hours, now a few, who meet for renewing of friendships and exchange of experiences, now the many, as each evening, when the entire company sits in the glow of the flaming logs. Then the little organ is brought out; Allen

Crawford plays accompaniments for camping lyrics written by John Murray Gibbon, and everybody sings!

The reason for being in Larch Valley became apparent on our first morning, when at nine o'clock a party of hikers, led by Walter Feuz, expert Swiss guide, set off, with fruit and sandwiches in their knapsacks, to make a round trip over Wastach Pass into Paradise Valley, returning by Sentinel Pass. Having no reputation for climbing to sustain, I watched them depart with great content.

An hour later another group set out, for a shorter battle with the heights. Then Dan and a young Canadian artist, Frank Panabaker, started off carrying sketch boxes, for a morning's work. After an interval I returned to my tepee and tried out the advantages of turning the head of my sleeping-bag around to where the foot had been. That simple act resolved into harmony all the differences between Mother Nature and myself. With a sense of complete happiness, I headed for the north end of the valley to look for alpine flowers, suspecting I might find many beside the falling waters of the brook, near its rocky ledges.

After a post-breakfast session around the fire, on our second morning in Larch Valley, Mr. Palenske and Dan, with their fishing tackle and sketching outfits, left for a day at Lake Moraine. ("All the way down, and all the

Wenkchemna Glacier

way up again," I thought.) Soon afterward, I joined a group led by John Murray Gibbon, to climb up the first reaches of Mount Temple. Among the good companions were Mrs. Peter Whyte, artist, and the wife of the president of the Sky Line Trail Hikers, who is himself an artist; and Mrs. Dan McCowan, who, in the midst of Rocky Mountain wildness, charms me by looking as though she were about to walk down Park Avenue.

Alpenstocks proved useful as we made our way over rocks and fallen trees and through low growth juniper. Mrs. Philip Moore found a specimen of rare plant and gathered it carefully to take back to Banff for Mr. Carl Rungius's alpine garden, while the rest of us were gathering other flowers. After awhile we all scattered and I found myself high up, far away, and alone. Looking from the height Lake Moraine could be seen, more than a thousand feet below, a green jewel gleaming in a dark setting.

That evening at the sing-song around the camp-fire, everyone was called upon, as usual, to contribute to the jollity of the occasion. I sat listening and laughing with the others, and while I was gazing upon the high mountains around us, there flashed a picture, made in my mind when I had been told a story at Banff some weeks earlier. It showed the then King Pradjodapok of Siam, a slim young man, riding with his party through the high passes of the Canadian Rockies, preceded by a pack train that included Oscar, head waiter of the Banff Springs Hotel. As the story went, Oscar had so pleased his Siamese Majesty, in the dining-room, that nothing would satisfy him except that the hotel management should release Oscar in order that this popular member of the hotel staff, who had never ridden a horse in his life, might accompany the Royal party and preside over the coffee making. A revolution in the routine of the hotel was arranged, and Oscar, having been hoisted onto the back of a horse, rode bravely out into the wilds. Oscar made good, rode the trail, came back, and was awarded a Trail Rider's button; but, I was told, several times when Oscar found himself unable to dismount, he suggested that the horse be shot under him as the easiest way of getting to the ground!

I had thought of Oscar with sympathy and admiration many times, especially at the end of my first day of trail riding along Brewster Creek; now, as memory brought King Pradjodapok before me, another flash was set off in my mind. I saw again a garden in New York City, and a lady walking the flowered alleys accompanied by the most engaging creature imaginable. I spoke; the lady gladly talked. She told me that King Pradjodapok had given her this cat, adding that it was worth five thousand dollars. Then she enlightened my ignorance about the breed of Siamese cat, by telling me

its extraordinary intelligence is the result of crossing a
cat and a monkey. As the lady passed on with her pet, I
had remained sitting on the bench long enough to write
about the incident.

Now, when my turn came to add to the camp-fire
program, I recited the lines I had written in a garden,
one sunny May morning three years before. Here they
are:

Lines to a Siamese Cat

A king of Siam was your foster-father,
A monkey was your great, great, great-grandmother,
You love all dogs, both good and bad,
But you harry cats till the cats go mad.
With eyes as blue as an April morn,
And a coat the colour of a gentle fawn,
Your nose, and your ears, your tail, and your toes,
Are dark as midnight, so everyone knows
That you are indeed, a Siamese cat,
Beautiful, expensive, and intelligent at that,
You come when you're called, and talk, and cry;
And wear a pretty harness with a bow to catch the eye.
Anyone can see your manners were taught you by a king
So forget your monkey ancestor, you lovely thing!

The fun and fellowship of our last evening sing-song
around the camp-fire culminated when Mrs. James
Simpson, gay as a girl, and Mr. Sam Ward, who had
already amused us mightily with his story-telling,

danced an Irish jig.

Looking across the darkened valley as we rose to go to our tepees for the night, I saw, above the fourth of the Ten Peaks, Jupiter glowing in the western sky.

That night, long after my companions had fallen asleep lost to sight under blankets, I lay thinking, warm and comfortable in my sleeping-bag. A tiny fire still burned upon the ground within reach of my hand; its rising and sinking flames cast dancing shadows on the canvas that walled us frailly in from surrounding immensities.

Above me I saw, shining from very far away, a star. Now and again through the stillness I heard the clank-clank of a bell as one of the grazing horses wandered near.

The fire-light sank to embers that winked sleepily; then all was dark. In the darkness the fiction of walls created by sight of the tepee's canvas no longer existed. I knew I was lying at the foot of Mount Temple alone under a starry sky, 7,000 feet above the sea.

The sea. I began to think myself down to it, from Larch Valley, 7,300 feet, to Moraine Lake, 6,200; to Lake Louise, 5,400; to Banff, 4,700; to Calgary, 3,400; until finally I was back at the old Connecticut studio, 500 feet above Long Island Sound—I was home—and remembered no more.

"Thank GOD," I exclaimed devoutly next morning upon opening my eyes to discover that blue sky was above us. Mrs. Wheeler, who had from the beginning been our fire commissioner, was leaning from out her down quilts a little more casually than the Blessed Damoselle leaned out of heaven. Looking over at me she asked, "Are you cold?"

"No," I replied, "merely happy." Mrs. Wheeler chuckled softly as she brushed a hand across her face. There was more smoke than flame to the tiny fire she was nursing with shreds of paper and a handful of wood chips. Aroused by the smoke Mrs. Simpson, too, sat up and reminded us that our duffle must be ready for the pack horses as soon as breakfast was finished.

A bright fire of three small logs was soon leaping up in the centre of our bedroom floor (!); the three of us determined to get up, and did so. It was six-forty-five A. M.

As for packing, it wouldn't take long to close my dressing bag that contained extra woollies, a first-aid kit, alcohol and cold cream to clean up with when water was too far away. Dan would look after the bedding; we had brought our own sleeping-bags, blankets and pillows—a fancy touch, pillows, but they are great conciliators when dealing with stubborn facts of earth. Never again would I carry along the heavy kapok sleeping-bags, having found out how much warmer, and lighter for the horses to carry, are the ones filled with eider-down. (They are expensive to buy, but may be hired.) Lighter for the horses—that's the end to aim at, I thought, as I opened the flap of the tepee and went out to join the crowd at the grub tent.

During this last day in camp many went hiking, but there was always a group of men around the camp-fire, holding on to the remaining hours of a companionship they might not enjoy again for a twelvemonth. With the sun pouring down, and a breeze now and again drifting smoke from the fire into their eyes, cronies sat side by side, pipes between their teeth, while they leaned against a log telling stories and gazing at the snowy peak of Mount Fay.

At intervals pack horses were driven in to camp, their racks empty, each to depart later with a load. I could see them from the north end of the valley where I sat in a sunny hollow of the mountainside, gazing at the Ten Peaks whose tops got tangled, now and then, in white clouds that came sailing across a sky of blue; or watching the crystal clear waters of the mountain stream falling over stones to the buffalo bush of the bottom, with Lyall larches above me, white heath near to my hand and many a fuzzy seed head of the alpine anemone.

Supper was served at five. Toward six o'clock, we set

Larch Valley, Camp of the Trail Hikers

out on the trail to Moraine Lake. How easy it seemed, going down, and beautiful at that time of early evening. We were at the Lodge in a little over an hour. Then came the Pow Wow, in the Community Room, with guests from Lake Louise present. The distinguished explorer, A. O. Wheeler, husband of my "room" mate, spoke on the topography and history of the area over which we had been hiking. When Mrs. James Simpson, my other recent "room" mate, was elected to the office of President of the Sky Line Trail Hikers, I felt very like a lady-in-waiting. Stories and lovely songs brought the program to an end.

Chateau Lake Louise. 11 P. M. August 6:—Could anything be more of a contrast to an Indian tepee than this apartment? Dan and I shall be here at Lake Louise for two days before leaving for the Pacific Coast. I want now to put down what is in my mind, before a new day brings new thoughts.

The Trail Ride of five days drew a line of dramatic episodes across the imagination, leaving an impression in the mind of wide and moving grandeur. The Trail Hike, with a settled base in the midst of magnificent mountains, gave opportunities for a deeper acquaintance with them, gave time for experience to be impressed upon the heart.

Out of the wind, and the rain, and the sunshine of

three days in Larch Valley, the word that remains is the word spoken to one alone, in the stillness of dawn, and the stillness of midnight at the foot of Mount Temple.

CHAPTER XXIII

EN ROUTE TO VANCOUVER

The Duchess's Diary

ON THE morning of our departure, I ran out of the Chateau for a last look at Lake Louise—the magnificent peaks and snowy Victoria Glacier lifted high above amethystine waters; the alpine garden along its margin where grow so many of the flowers I made friends with in the high reaches of Og Pass; then back to Dan and the piled luggage.

When the bus came in, Mr. John Meredith, manager of this, to me, perfect hotel, and his assistant, Mr. Mackay, both of whom had shown us every courtesy during our three visits to the Chateau this summer, saw us off with good wishes for our journey to the Coast. Again, we were being swept out to the unknown even while the tide of travel was sweeping lucky ones in, to the shores of this loveliest of lakes.

Away we went, out of the Chateau grounds, by a motor road beside a mountain stream, soon passing the road to Lake Moraine; catching sight of fine scenery all the way until at the end of three miles we were half a thousand feet lower than when we started, feeling warm sunlight, seeing bright flower borders of the Canadian Pacific Station terrace stirring in the cool mountain air. There were a few minutes to wait and, as we sat on the station platform in the sunshine, I thought of the marvels of engineering skill that had flung steel across chasms and forced it through mountains to create this Canadian Pacific Railway. I recalled the extreme care of the track which Dan and I have noted all along from Montreal, and suddenly my imagination began dealing with the track that lay ahead— the Spiral Tunnels, the trestles, and snow-sheds—then I heard Dan say, "Here she comes," and, looking up, saw the twelve-car train sliding smoothly up to the station platform.

Greeted by a smiling Negro porter, a homey feeling came over me as we stepped aboard. Our compartment proved to be near the end of the train; it didn't take us a minute to settle our things and get into seats in the outside section of the observation car.

As train No. 13 begins to move out of the station, Dan and I wave good-bye to Lake Louise. . . . For the second time we are making the trip to Field. We cross the ubiquitous Bow River, and it leaves us. . . . Now Bath Creek runs along beside the track. How lucky we are to have such a day—bright sunshine, cool air all about us as we sit out of doors seeing Ptarmigan Peak and Mount Hector towering into the blue sky ahead. We miss Sally—God bless her old front tires—but I am glad that Dan is free today to look about as much as he likes. . . . The train is climbing . . . it arrives at the Great Divide and stops.

"We're on top of the world, Duchess," Dan exclaims, as he hurries off with a lot of passengers. I stay where I can watch the scene from the side of this car. Cameras are popping like corn over a fire, all directed toward a rustic arch above a little stream which, believe it or not, flows two ways. It is thrilling to know one is looking at the same time upon the very backbone of the continent, the place where the dividing line is drawn between Alberta and British Columbia, and the spot where the railroad reaches its highest point. I know, as I look at those two dividing streams, that the one which flows eastward will finally reach Hudson's Bay and the Atlantic Ocean, and the one that flows westward will soon become Wapta Lake and then, as the Kicking Horse River, run away and away till it joins the mighty Columbia, to pour at last into the Pacific Ocean. . . . Back come the passengers. A granite shaft on the left of the track is in memory of Sir James Hector the discoverer of Kicking Horse Pass, through which we are about to travel. His discovery made crossing the Rockies possible. All aboard!

Down grade to Stephen, B.C. Now we are in Yoho National Park, and I think of Yoho Valley as I have seen it. . . . Cataract Creek comes pouring down to the left of the train, and near it begins the trail to Lake O'Hara which Dan points out to me. . . . Then we both turn our gaze to the right and see that the train is skirting the south shore of Lake Wapta. On the lake's further shore is the Chalet Bungalow Camp where many people stay to enjoy the trout fishing.

Written later:—"Dan," I said, "we will soon be at the first Spiral Tunnel, and I hate tunnels, even when they are straight."

"The answer is lunch. Come along," he replied, and we went swaying through the Pullmans to emerge at last into a cheerful dining-car.

After being shown to a table on the right, next to windows that gave one a marvellous view, we ordered luncheon, and the white-coated waiter moved off.

Gazing out of the window Dan said: "We are now in Kicking Horse Pass. When Sir James Hector was on the expedition which brought discovery of this way through the Rocky Mountains, he got a kick in the chest from the heels of a vicious horse."

"And so," I broke in, "the pass was named for the horse instead of for Hector. Funny, isn't it? But, it's the way of the world. That kick was more dramatic than the bruise it made, and drama wins the crowd."

"You really are melancholy over the approaching tunnels, aren't you Duchess? Well, cheer up, here comes the chow."

"But just think, Dan," I insisted, "in a moment or two there will be ten thousand feet of Cathedral Mountain right above the roof of this car, and it will continue to stay there while we travel more than a mile. Why! My mind is doing a spiral now that would put the tracks to shame if they could understand." Dan laughed and, as our waiter placed before us the first course, switched his attention away from the bread and butter, saying:

"In twenty hours we shall be at the Pacific Coast—where the salmon run. Doesn't that thrill you, Duchess? And when I consider how I'm going to pull 'em in!"

Blackout! Windows disappear. Electric lights come on. I concentrate upon food and conversation.

"How easy it would be, Dan, for old Mother Nature to turn over in her sleep. If she should, these tunnels would fold up as easily as an evening newspaper."

The waiter changed plates, serving the second course.

"I wouldn't be cursed with an imagination like yours for a good deal. Now," said Dan, putting a whacking slice of broiled beefsteak on my plate, "eat your lunch. You'll soon feel better." And I did, for at that moment the train emerged from tunnel darkness.

"Oh! the blessed daylight!" I exclaimed, gazing eagerly through the glass of the window—and caught, upon the second, a marvellous view.

"Look, Dan, quickly—way across to the north." But I needn't have spoken, for he'd seen it as soon as I had, the far Yoho Valley open to the sky, coming down in glorious colour to meet the valley which our train was crossing, that of the foaming Kicking Horse River.

"Yoho! indeed!" Dan exclaimed; and after a moment, "the Indian word for astonishment is certainly the right name."

Memory of all the good times we had enjoyed in Yoho Valley swept over me. I might even have become sentimental about Yoho had not there come at that instant another blackout of windows, and a flooding of electric light that changed our mood as we entered the tunnel under Mount Ogden.

"Yesterday I read all about this part of the trip, Dan," I said as we continued luncheon. "Ever since the Great Divide the track has been descending—soon it will be twelve hundred feet. The engine has been playing tag with the observation car, looping the loop at the same time, through two mountains, and chasing the raging Kicking Horse River. I should call the twelve miles from Hector to Field a sublime geographical three-ring circus." This amused Dan. Then, in the midst of all the immensities, a polite waiter offered us Canadian Edam

Fraser River and the old Cariboo Trail

cheese. I always go Roman when in Rome, so now I was in the act of complying, when to my great content our train rushed out into the full light of day.

As he put two lumps of sugar into his coffee cup, Dan remarked:

"Now that we have passed through the Spiral Tunnels, I'd like to say, Duchess, that you do not take them seriously enough. They are among the most notable engineering feats in existence."

"They are magnificent!" I exclaimed laughing with pleasure, "the finest tunnels a girl ever left behind her!"

On our way up to the dining-car the names lettered on the doors of the Pullman cars had amused me; now, returning to the end of the train, I read all these names over again, and, as soon as I reached a desk, I jotted them down for a souvenir. Here they are:

> Argyle, and Riverton,
> Nanette, Red Deer;
> Saugeen and Sudbury,
> Ignace, Windemere;
> Albion and Fesseferne,
> And last of all Kathleen.
> But last of all is best of all
> And fairest ever seen,

when you've been swaying and clutching the backs of seats as you make your way through a long train to the observation car at the end.

I'd no sooner finished writing this than I felt the train slowing, and in a moment it stopped at Field.

Sight of the old platform brings back all the fun this summer in which Field has been a link. Before I can get out for a walk, men come into the car carrying pails filled with big chunks of ice, to replenish the water coolers. I know that there is to be a fifteen-minute stop here while the whole train is given a look-over, so out I go. . . .

Again in our section: The porter comes to me as I seat myself and says:

"Set your watch back an hour, Ma'am; we change here from Mountain time to Pacific time." I thank him, amused to see through the windows all the promenading passengers scuttling to get aboard. I feel the car vibrate as oilers and mechanics outside walk along close to the car trucks, knocking things here and there, and poking long-nosed oil-cans into dark spaces. (The well-being of all of us is tied up with those knockings and pokings; they make me feel safe.)

Having twiddled the hands of my watch until they register eleven-forty A. M., I think to myself, "An hour that has already been spent is mine to spend over again!" This is exciting, because, to me, time is as tangible as a length of gold-shot damask.

All but imperceptibly our train begins to move out of Field station. . . . Now we are passing the yards—the round-house—where a few weeks ago I clambered about with Mr. Ross, Superintendent. . . . Kicking Horse River seems to have gone all tame; it is spreading in streamlets over a wide bottom. . . . But that was only for a minute; the river is gathering again into a deep channel, logs and tree trunks along its banks tell of the swirling waters of Spring.

Standing motionless on a sandy point that juts into the waters of the Kicking Horse River, I suddenly see a great brown bear!

12:20 P. M.:—I've been asleep! A pretty way to spend twenty minutes of my recaptured hour. And while I wasn't looking, the mountains have grown smaller, forested now to their summits. How good the cottonwood trees beside us look. Temperature has risen; the warmth feels strange. . . .

12:30 P. M.:—Sitting beside Dan on the right-hand side of the open observation car at end of train. All seats around us are filled. Many of the men and women are holding cameras.

Sunlight glancing from foliage of trees we are passing fills the surrounding scene with colour, and, together with the strong, pure air all about us as we sit out of doors, is giving me and no doubt everyone here a gorgeous sense of happiness.

"Look, Duchess," Dan says suddenly, "up there above us winding around the cliffs—the new scenic Kicking Horse motor road. Next year we'll be driving along it with Sally." I give the road a flick of the eye, but it is the engine far ahead that I watch; it is pulling the twelve links of our train along the wild bank of a wild river, sending out from below as it labours forward great puffs of white steam, and at the same time from its stack shooting yellowish smoke up into the clear air above. This is glorious. . . .

An abrupt turn west. . . . Leanchoil— We stop on a siding. I hear the sound of an approaching eastbound train; it must have two engines. Yes, there they are! old 5772 and 5911. It gives me a thrill to recognize their numbers as they rush by breathing like racehorses and pulling a long string of cars.

"There must be a lot of people on that train," says our conductor, who happens to be standing in the aisle near us; "it's got three diners."

Palliser is left behind. The scenery now becomes dramatic. Kicking Horse River close beside us goes headlong through a narrow gorge . . . that deepens. . . . Vertical mountain walls each side of us grow higher and higher, hemming us in. And all the while sound of the river roaring as it lunges from side to side of the narrow canyon reverberates like rolling thunder. Everyone is excited.

Dan and I, looking way ahead, see our engine and first three cars curving along the edge of fighting waters. Suddenly everything is blotted out in a tunnel. Daylight again. The river bank, along which we are running slowly, is so heavily reinforced the Kicking Horse must here kick especially hard. How glorious it all is!

Glenogle—As the train enters a third tunnel, Dan and I guess what the river will be doing when we come out. . . . Dan wins! The river has flung itself over to the left again. It would be more correct to say the engineer has flung us over to the right! . . .

Wide are the waters now, and blue the ranging mountains as our train comes out of the shadowed grandeur of the Kicking Horse Canyon into the full light of day at Golden. Slowing to a stop among many tracks where another long passenger train, and freight cars unescorted by any engine, are standing. Oil-tanks.

Prosaic to look at—this railway yard—yet I suppose right now there are flowing through it the romance of mines, and of mills, and of the fertile acres of Columbia River Valley. . . . An eastbound train passes; at once our train starts, gathering speed as it heads west for the long lap to the railway's next divisional point, Revelstoke.

"Gosh, what a valley!" exclaims Dan. We are gazing upon lush green lands through which, bearing gifts, a generous river is flowing. There are willow trees, and plantations of potatoes in bloom, and wheat, acres of it, standing, and cut, and in sheaves that men are loading upon horse-drawn carts. To the west, framing in the scene, amethystine mountain peaks are shining in a cloudless sky. Excitedly putting his sketch-book back into his pocket, Dan says to me:

"Tie on your bonnet, Duchess! From now until sunset we're going to look upon a world that will make your pencil and mine lie right down and give up their jobs."

Foot-hills rise from the wide lush valley of the Columbia to verdant peaks that notch a radiant sky. . . .

As our train crosses Blaeberry River I see a group of white tents—used I suppose by the road workers; they look good to me. . . .

Donald—And now we cross the Columbia River that has been sweeping grandly along beside us all the way from Golden. The eastern thrust, and cloud-dappled peaks of the Selkirks—what a glorious background for the picture made by this river rushing now at the foot of tree-clad cliffs, between steep canyon walls.

A mountain torrent from heights above us falls whitely, cascading down a cleft rock face to the very tracks that span its waters. I can feel around me the excitement of the passengers. . . . Wider and wider grows the Columbia, largest but one of all rivers in Western America.

Aromatic fragrance of balsam pervades the air all around the twenty of us who sit in the open section of the observation car at the train's end; (it even permeated the closed car I was walking through a moment ago and made me run to get out here in time to breathe to the full its vital sweetness). I've marked the area—between Donald and Beavermouth—with the word BALSAM, that next time I may not miss even one minute of the full forest fragrance. . . . As our train follows the curving, tumultuous slate-grey river, spruce and pine in serried ranks rise stiffly from water's edge to the very sky above us.

2:10 P. M.:—Our train slows to a stop at Beavermouth, most northern point of the railroad; a grove of trees near this car on our right, and far away to the southwest rise guardian mountains. Columbia River that we have been following for an hour disappears around a spur of the Selkirk Range. There is a climb ahead of us of 1,300 feet to reach the summit. Two engines now are pulling our long train as we begin the ascent. The Beaver River comes pouring down toward us—almost upon us!

Beaver River Canyon—This is glorious. Toward us, over great boulders beside which we are climbing, falls a swirling, yellow-green, white-crested mass of tumbling waters! And the trees! . . . . Sixty-six miles from Field we cross the Beaver River, climbing rapidly.

Rogers—Three miles further along our train runs across a bridge, spanning Mountain Creek, whose waters are 150 feet below us! The flying trapeze is nothing compared with this Canadian Pacific Railway!

We're in Glacier Park! Sunlight pours out from behind great white clouds upon a world of marvellous beauty. Balsam fragrance fills the air, and sight of the sheer sweep of green earth, from sky to the far bottom, is breath-taking! Dan and I turn toward each other to express our feelings and find we have no words, so continue in silence to gaze upon the glorious scene.

Sturdee—A gap between shoulders of mountains gives us a memorable vista of misty blue ranges far away. The engine whistles a kind of living groan (no flesh and blood racehorses have anything on this breed of iron mountain-climber). In front of a house near the tracks a little child dressed in red and another in blue stand watching the passing of our long train. What do they do here in winter? . . . . Close on our right are splendid forest trees—pines whose fingers seem to reach out to us, white cedar, and larch. . . . A silver thread of water falling, as if from heaven, past us to a depth below, undiscernible. (Tracks are double here.)

From the marvellous height at which the train is now running, suddenly far below there opens to our sight a mighty basin of the Beaver River, threaded with channels that in spring must flood all that now is dry. . . .

Agassiz, B.C.

Cutbank—

Surprise Creek bridge—The beauty of the view from here, and the fact that the steel structure our train is passing over at this point is 170 feet above the creek's waters bring a catch in my throat. Never shall I forget what I am seeing today. . . . And still the wonders continue.

Stony Creek bridge—Oh-o-o-! Ahead I cannot see the structure by which we are passing over—we seem to have left the mountainside and to be floating as a dirigible in circumambient air—but looking back as the track curves, the splendid trestle work becomes visible, an achievement of engineering which spans this chasm at the one and only possible point, and at a height of 270 feet above the creek's downward-rushing waters! (I wonder how much more excitement of this kind I can stand?) . . . . Here we are safely at Stony Creek Station. I sigh with relief and delight. After coming to a stop, the train moves on again, leaving Engine No. 5776 on a side track. Willows and heavenly red cedars close beside our way. The red cedar trees are beautiful beyond words. . . . The conductor comes out to us and calls:

"All inside, if you please. We are about to enter the famous Connaught Tunnel."

CHAPTER XXIV

TOWARD THE SUNSET

DAN and I hurry into the closed observation car ahead. Lights come on as the train plunges into darkness. (Written later.) I read, first, about the tunnel, learned it was named for the Duke of Connaught who was Governor General of Canada when the tunnel was opened in 1916. It is over 5 miles from portal to portal. Its construction shortened the East to West trip by 4½ miles and reduced the height of the tracks by 552 feet. The tunnel is 29 feet wide, 21½ feet from rails to ceiling, is double tracked and lined with cement. With this information clear in my mind, I had a picture of us shuttling through Mount MacDonald, at the summit of the Selkirks, and knew that at the end of fifteen minutes we would come out into daylight on their western slope. And suddenly, as it seemed, we did that very thing, the train stopping near a tower in which big fans are operated to keep the air of the tunnel always fresh; there was an entire absence of dust and gas as our train passed through.

3:25 P. M. Glacier:—One alights here for Glacier

National Park. To be within sight of it and not get off
the train is strange, when for years I have wished to see
Glacier Park's austere loveliness, its peaks and glaciers
and the Nakimu Caves of Cougar Valley, but above all
its forests of ancient trees.

The great Illicilliwaet Glacier, framed in dark forest
trees and scarred by crevasses, is visible from the train;
and, as we again move forward, verdant domes rise one
beyond another on the right side of the way, while
bracken clothes the banks.

Way up ahead, we can see the engine taking us along
the turgid glacial river of the big name, Illicilliwaet.
Beside us are trees that impress themselves upon the
heart. Clear of all disease, and free of undergrowth, they
stand glorious.

Again the train crosses the Illicilliwaet River, which
makes a big loop and then comes pouring back beside
the very tracks. There is a sudden darkening of daylight
as the train passes under crossed beams of snow-sheds and
over a steel bridge.

More of the glorious red cedars with their drooping
lacy branches. I wish I could indicate the wonder of this
forest that is beside us. . . . Looking back the way we
have come the view is enchanting. We are experiencing
a steady pressure of beauty. . . . Snow-sheds again.
. . . Tunnel. . . . More sheds. This part of the track
to Vancouver might be called "An Engineer's Night-

mare." Tunnel— Illicilliwaet keeps pouring madly down
beside us. . . . Again we go under the crossed beams of
snow-sheds. (The cost of constructing all this kind of
thing and then keeping it in first-class condition must
be terrific.)

Trees! The Trees! They make me want to "go her-
mit," and come here to live with them. And Illicilliwaet
pouring west is now a foaming pathway between curving green walls that our train is following.

Illicilliwaet Station—This marks the western boundary of Glacier National Park. The train does not stop.
Looking across the river I see new construction—work-
men's tents, huts. This is Downy—I remember reading
about a new piece of roadbed being constructed here to
increase the safety of the tracks. On temporary tracks
freight cars are, apparently, being used as living quarters. It would be amusing to turn a freight car into a
summer cottage.

Written later:—We reached Albert Canyon at four-
seventeen P. M. The train stopped ten minutes so that
everyone could see the beautiful spectacle. As we hurried out of doors onto the sunny platform, we were met
by a tonic freshness of mountain air and sight of flowers cascading down green terraces. Hurrying with the
others to a platform especially built, Dan and I were
met by a sight of wooded crags from which descended
walls of solid rock straight down for 150 feet to nar-

row, plunging, pent-up waters of the Illicilliwaet. . . .
Again on board, our train goes forward.

The sun, though hidden some of the time this afternoon, has brightened the scenes spread before us. . . .

We come to a marvellous stand of cottonwood trees,
mountain ash, and the, to me, always supremely beautiful red cedar. This is the vicinity of Revelstoke National Park. Mount McKenzie rises to the south. . . . I
must have fallen asleep. The train is standing in Revelstoke Station. Change of altitude, we're down to a mere
1,667 feet. Looking out I see a plantation of bright
flowers above a green bank, and crowds of passengers
promenading in the sunshine. It is five-ten P. M. I'll
hurry out.

Written later:—Looking down the long platform I
saw Dan's head above all the other heads, and I met him
in the station lunch room, where I went to buy fruit,
and he to get a newspaper. Suddenly we heard, "All
aboard," and, together with everyone else, hurried back
into the train, brightened up by the fifteen-minute
promenade.

Dan opened his paper, all set for news, and found it
was only the "boiler plate" section of next Sunday's
edition!

"Well, never mind," said philosophical Dan, as the
train moved out of the station, "here's something about
Revelstoke National Park." In a moment or two he

summed up for me what he had read, as follows:

Revelstoke Park, 100 miles square, is on top of a mountain, and includes Mount Revelstoke as well as the Clachnacudainn Range (the Scots have been busy around here!) and is reached by a hard road of easy grades through virgin forest! The road, says Dan with his eye on the pamphlet, winds along rocky ledges and on the verge of deep chasms. (Shades of Og Pass!) From the top one has a glorious view of the towering Selkirks on one side and the Monashee Mountains on the other, while the Columbia and the Illicilliwaet, like silver ribbons, intertwine about the city of Revelstoke.

"Now I ask you," says Dan, looking at me, "have we missed the finest bit of British Columbia by not camping out in Revelstoke Park?"

"Never mind what's past. Look at what's coming," I answered, and together we gazed through the wide windows of the observation car upon the smiling valley of Columbia River, enclosed by verdant mountains. Far against the sky snowy peaks glistened in the afternoon sunlight.

The Illi—being also cilli—what? or more clearly, Illicilliwaet—has lost itself in the Columbia. Imagine running all the breakneck miles from Golden only to throw yourself away at last! In peaceful bottom land hay is stacked where big horses are grazing. . . . The train crosses the wide Columbia . . . and we find ourselves among the Monashee Mountains.

Magnificent white pines! Growing on the sloping banks beside our way, golden-rod and bracken. It is these trees I shall remember; to live with them would make one godlike. . . .

Nearly an hour has passed. I have watched the train slowly descending through deep Eagle Pass. The tracks have been close to the edge of the water, laid in cuts made in the mountainsides.

We are now in the narrow valley of the Tonkawatla River. . . . The train climbs to Eagle Pass, 1,820 feet altitude. I see a sign, Clanwilliam; we do not stop. Off to the south-east Mount MacPherson rises. . . . Six miles further along, Three Valley. It is six P. M. Ten miles and we reach Taft. And now lovely Crazy Creek comes pouring down the cliff beside us, to run beneath the tracks and then into Eagle River, which our train is now following. . . . Four miles along, Cragellachie, the scene of the completion of the railway tracks from the east and the west. Here the Last Spike was driven home, uniting the two ends of the great transcontinental system. Our train does not stop, but I see from the window an obelisk which marks the place where the historic act occurred—on November 7, 1885. The first transcontinental train went through on June 28, 1886. And here we are today. It is now six-twenty-three P. M. Dan and I have been gazing upon a succession of natural wonders

[219]

and magnificent scenery since noon.

As we follow the valley of the Eagle River a farm-house flashes into view, and near it I see a boy milking a white cow. He turns to watch our train pass and waves a hand to us—little boy alone in a wide landscape at the day's end.

Still descending, our train slows to a stop at Sicamous Station then immediately goes on. If we had heeded the advice of friends who have made this trip, Dan and I would now be getting off here to spend the night at the hotel (under the same roof with the station). The scenery between Sicamous and Vancouver they say is magnificent. Going through tonight we shall miss see-ing it, but we plan to take a morning train on the way home, and then we shall see the great Frazer and Thompson River canyons. The Sicamous Hotel is on the very edge of Shuswap Lake. Now looking ahead (we are still in the observation car) I see dark wooded prom-ontories cutting the wide waters. Hazy ranging moun-tains show against a serene sky in which float golden clouds. Our way follows the curving shore of the lake.

As the altitude declined today after leaving Field, I no-ticed that my appetite, lost for a month in the high alti-tudes, was coming back. Tonight, at this moment, I am really hungry; and good it seems, after so long a time. Dan suggests going to the dining-car and I agree with pleasure.

Yale, on the Fraser River

Sunset glory is tinging clouds that float near the silvery first quarter of the August moon; the moon is hanging straight up and down in a turquoise sky. . . . On the inland side of our way, kindly, verdant mountainsides slope upward; the windows of cottages along the shore of Lake Sushwap shine as squares of light. . . . I see a mare with her foal grazing in deep, green grass, while a calf follows near them. . . . A farmstead, and sheep grazing in the twilight.

Forty minutes since we passed Sicamous Station. Sunset has gone to meet the coming night. We reach Salmon Arm Station. A long arm, indeed. . . .

Tappan—I can barely make out the name of the station in the gathering darkness. With all the beauty of forest and mountains I have looked upon since eleven o'clock this morning . . . I . . . am . . . going . . . to . . . sleep.

August 12, 4:45 A. M.:—Looking through my window, I see that the day seems to be doing business; all the trees are standing up, and everything, including the sky, as usual. . . .

7:00 A. M.:—Dan beat me to the dining-car by one minute. There at six-ten we ate a delicious breakfast. It's fine to be hungry. Now we're all set for Vancouver (at 7:45) and a good time.

[221]

Written later:—Twenty hours after we left Lake Louise, Dan and I stepped off *The Dominion*, into golden sunshine on the platform of the station at Vancouver. From an amazing variety of bags, suitcases, and hatboxes, which had been speedily ranged along the platform by the dark-skinned train porter, we claimed our own luggage; and then, accompanied by an elderly Oriental station porter wheeling a piled hand truck, we walked to a freight elevator where we were invited to ride up to street level with our possessions. The porter, removing a heavy cap, mopped his perspiring brow; and indeed the temperature seemed high to us, so lately in zero weather at Mount Assiniboine.

Whirled quickly by a taxi up to the dark brown pile of the Hotel Vancouver, I noticed as we entered its cool Victorian spaciousness that a clock said eight-fifteen A. M. "It is still a fine young day," I thought to myself.

As we were settling our belongings in an apartment perfectly suited to Dan's proportions, I remarked:

"It's too bad we ordered our mail sent straight on to Victoria, because we shall have to follow it, and I should like to stay here for awhile. Everything is just the way I like it."

"Then it is better for your soul that we move along," said Dan with a grin.

After an early lunch we set out to see the city of Vancouver, visiting, first, several excellent department stores where we purchased some needed articles. Then we sank into seats in a big bus and were taken through Stanley Park, past English Bay, and around the Marine Drive, growing more and more enthusiastic. The sight of luxuriant flowers and shrubs, after all the forests we have been looking at lately, filled me with delight. The bus returned through Chinatown and the business section, so altogether we gathered a fair impression of this likable city that is only fifty years old and yet presents an appearance of maturity and modern efficiency.

CHAPTER XXV

VANCOUVER HARBOUR

I HAD a yen to see Vancouver harbour. When I suggested to the Duchess that she go along, she said that she had something so very important to do that it would take her all the afternoon. This was her way of saying: "Smells, fish, cold, damp. No thank you."

To me any seaport is an exciting place full of romantic possibilities. Leaving the Duchess to her very important work, I hurried to the Information Desk and asked Miss Foster, as I called her, what could be done about seeing the harbour; was there a steamer that would take me around? There was, and it would be leaving at two-thirty. If I caught the right street car and remembered what turns to make after I got off it, I might be able to catch the boat. "But," said Miss Foster, smiling cheerfully, "you'll have to hurry."

Lady Luck is a friend of mine. The first street car that came along was the right one, and I didn't miss a turn in walking to the dock. After buying my ticket I found the *Harbour Prince* and went aboard; she was about ready to leave.

Good brown smells—of coffee, spices, and tarred rope —hung in the air. Across the slip was a big fish-packing house; trawlers had just arrived with holds full of salmon, of halibut from Alaska, of great crabs in huge baskets. Floating around in the water, beside this and that, was an old spar covered with barnacles that, if given a chance, would have spun a tall yarn.

Anchored in the harbour and at their docks were ships from the seven seas—great liners in from the Orient, from Australia, from New Zealand. Exciting? Nothing like it! Just as I lighted my pipe the whistle of the *Harbour Prince* gave a toot and she backed out into the harbour. Where we were going I had not the slightest idea, and didn't much care; my pipe was drawing well and, as far as I could see, the only passengers were the Captain's friend, now with him in the wheel-house, three or four persons on the after deck, and myself. This boat was so small I thought it might have a good old gong and jingle in the engine room, but I learned she was right up to date when a telegraph signal sounded full speed ahead.

We seemed to be going up-stream away from the harbour and all the ships that I had come to see, which was puzzling; but, comfortable up in the bow, my pipe reloaded, I felt ready for anything. "The *Harbour Prince*," I thought, "is on her regular run and will probably turn up in Vancouver again this evening, so what?"

For two days there had been a fire on the north shore of the harbour. The Duchess was afraid that it was a forest fire and that the great trees she so loved would be destroyed. But on inquiring about it, I learned that a logging crew were burning the slashing on cut-over land, and the consequence was that land and water for miles were enveloped in a wonderful blue haze.

As our steamer went under a railroad bridge, the Captain leaned from the pilot house to see that we made a safe passage and did not bump anything. The C.P.R. tracks were on our right and, between the tracks and water, on a narrow strip of land, fishermen's houses were packed close together for a mile or more. Some of them were so flimsy they looked as though a passing train would shake them into the river, but all of their gay yards were brilliant with flowers.

The Captain and the Lady in the wheel-house continued to chatter like a couple of magpies.

Then everything flattened out. It looked as though the trip was going to be a washout, and I thought to myself, "The Duchess will have the laugh on me."

Just as I was beginning to feel that Lady Luck had fooled me, the boat swung hard to port and headed up a narrow passage, apparently making for a landing that appeared on a point of land ahead. The Captain's friend came out of the pilot house and descended to the deck where I was standing. "This must be the end of the trip for her," I thought.

As the *Harbour Prince* slid up the dock, the lady went over the side and made a flying leap, landed on the pier as gracefully as a dancer. With a wave of her hand, and "Many thanks, see you later," she ran up the pier.

Now fantastic things began to happen to the scenery as I looked ahead. The smoke from the fire on the north shore enveloped everything; the sun was a copper ball; the shadows on the left-hand shore were so blue that to think of them in terms of paint seemed absurd, while the opposite shore shone like burnished gold in the sunlight. And all the beauty I gazed at was doubled by its own reflection in motionless waters. On a point of land ahead under a great cliff appeared a marble palace gleaming like a huge pearl. The shadows from four arches in its façade glowed like sapphires in the water below them. I looked up at the wheel-house of this fairy ship that I was travelling on, fully expecting to see that some Genie had taken charge. But there was the same Captain leaning out of a window smoking his pipe. He waved to me and called: "Come on up; you can see better here." So up I went and then turned to look about me. The spell was broken, the palace was only a hydro-electric plant built of concrete.

"You fooled me this afternoon," I said turning to the Captain. "I had expected to see something of the harbour." With a chuckle he replied:

"You saw a bit of it coming up. But isn't this pretty nice?"

"I should say it is, and so near a big city, too. As a matter of fact, how far are we from Vancouver?"

"Well, when we get to the end of the run, at Wigwam Inn, we'll be about twenty-five miles from the city. When we left Vancouver," he continued, "we came up Burrad Inlet; and when I swung the steamer over to port we entered what is called Indian Arm."

"Wasn't that a kind of park, where your lady friend got off?" I asked.

"Yes, Belcarra Park—great place for picnics. Lots of people come out from the city to spend the day there."

"By the way," I said, laughing, "you didn't slow up much when your friend got off."

"She's been around boats a lot," the Captain answered, smiling, "and when there are no other passengers for the Park, like this afternoon, she always says: 'Don't bother to stop. Just put her alongside, and I'll hop off.' You see," he went on, "her husband is chief engineer on one of the big C.P.R. liners. She told me on the way up here this afternoon that she was worried about him, because his ship is over at Shanghai, and things are bad in China these days."

"Well, she made a pretty landing."

"Yes," he laughed, "she's right clever around the water."

Cadboro Yacht Club, Vancouver Island

We were now passing what the Captain told me was Crocker Island. When we reached its far end I saw a dock and the Wigwam Inn. This was the end of the trip. As we drew in alongside the dock the Captain said:

"We don't leave for the return trip until six o'clock, so you'll have plenty of time to look around. They serve a right good meal at the Inn, if you happen to get hungry."

Taking the Captain at his word I went to the Wigwam Inn and looked around its attractive rooms. There I picked up a copy of the *Legend,* written by Jane Parkin, which told how the nearby Falls acquired their name, the Falls of the Spray of Pearls. Getting the gist of the story as I went along, I visited the waterfall and, looking around me at the scene, tried to imagine young Norman McNabb and his lovely bride, Pearl, in this setting, eighty years ago. By the time I had seen the wonders of Cathedral Canyon, and had got back to the Inn, I was ready for something to eat.

Beside a big window in the dining-room of Wigwam Inn, where I could look out on the water, I sat down and ordered dinner. Looking out of the window now, I saw a salmon jumping, and I heard the waitress at my elbow ask, "What will you have for dessert, sir?"

At that very moment a great salmon came clean out of water and in my excitement I answered, "Deep fish waffle fly."

The girl's sense of humour got the better of her, and she laughed right out as I untangled the line into "deep dish apple pie." When the pie and coffee brought a good dinner to an end, I hurried out and watched the waters of Salmon Arm until, at a little after six o'clock, the *Harbour Prince,* with a toot of her whistle, started on the return trip to Vancouver.

In the evening light the shores and the serene waters were even more beautiful than they had been in the afternoon, for now the setting sun was casting long purple shadows. I was up in the wheel-house with the Captain. The steamer was passing Crocker Island when a canoe shot out from the shadowy shore.

"Got a passenger," remarked the Captain as he signalled the engineer to slow down. The canoe with two men in it came alongside; it had an outboard motor. One man jumped aboard, and the other, left in the canoe, tried to start the motor, which had been shut off.

"No! Not that way!" yelled our new passenger, gesticulating wildly. "Give her some gas! No! Don't pour it on: use the throttle!" While he had been shouting, the canoe had drifted away from the steamer and now disappeared as we rounded a bend. Coming up to the wheel-house the man threw down his hat, saying:

"That fellow will never learn to run a motor! Well, he can paddle back."

I learned that he, like many Vancouver men, lived on a motor boat in summer and went back to the city only when it was necessary. In talking with him, it amused me to learn that what was taking him back to Vancouver now was that he might be ready for a golf tournament in the morning, and I knew just how he felt. His big cabin cruiser, with several persons on deck, was riding at anchor in a little bay. As we were passing it a pantomime took place. In response to the waving on the deck of his boat, our passenger pointed back to where he had met the steamer, and then went through the motions of paddling a canoe. Apparently his friends got the meaning, because they all began to laugh and show their amusement. Darkness was beginning to settle on the waters.

Far ahead I saw boats putting out from shore; others in midstream were setting out great nets with lights fastened to them.

"Salmon nets," said the Captain, "and sometimes the fishermen don't bother to put lights on them. If you get one of those things under your stern there's the devil to pay."

Someone was standing up in a small boat, waving a lantern as we approached Balcarra Park. The *Harbour Prince* slowed down and the Captain's friend of the morning came aboard and ran up to the wheel-house.

The three of us fell into conversation about boats big

and little, and water, smooth and rough. It was dark now; the only light came from the binnacle. This guide of all ships fascinated the lady and she talked very knowingly of navigation. Turning to me she said, "Bet you don't know what course we're on now."

I don't know a thing about navigation, less about dead reckoning, and the only star in the whole universe that I can recognize is the North Star; but I have a strong sense of direction. As it happened, at the moment I was sitting by a window, and, thus challenged, I looked out, wondering if my old friend the North Star was about. There it was, as ever on the job, with its faithful friend at hand. Guessing at the angle made by the steamer, I announced that the *Harbour Prince* was sailing due southwest. This brought a merry peal of laughter from the lady, who remarked that she would hate to trust a ship to my navigation. Then turning to the Captain she said, "Tell the gentleman the course."

The Captain looked down at the compass. "Due southwest," he announced with a laugh. The lady turned on me.

"How did you know?" she asked, and added that I was a brute.

Our little steamer passed neatly under the railroad bridge and soon nosed her way into the dock at Vancouver. There was a round of cordial good-byes and then I jumped ashore and headed for the hotel. It seemed a week since I'd left. "The Duchess is an unpredictable woman," I thought to myself; "I wonder what she has been doing?"

CHAPTER XXVI

GOING PLACES WITHOUT SALLY

The Duchess's Diary

LONGING for an afternoon among trees and flowers, and knowing Dan was off for Vancouver Harbour and all the watery things he loves, I went to the Information Desk in Hotel Vancouver to ask a pleasant young woman in charge how to get to Stanley Park.

"Walk to Pinder Street," she said, "and take car number ten, going west."

Nothing could be simpler. When I got to Pinder Street I found four corners and shining car tracks raying in as many directions. As I paused to consider where to go, I suddenly remembered that common carriers have become superior, and stop where they please. One might have lived all one's life on a certain street and seen the motorman grow up to manhood, yet, if his tram didn't happen to like uneven numbers, it would go past one's corner without ever stopping to put one off or take one up. And then the matter of where these common carriers stop—would it be, I wondered, here in Vancouver, the far corner or the near corner? And,

[234]

above all, which way was west? Really this matter of taking a tram to the park was not so simple. But of course! A mere question addressed to the man at the paper stand near by would solve my problem.

"Stanley Park?" I asked with a smile and a rising inflection. The busy man waved a hand in the general direction of the corner opposite to the one on which I had been standing. I thanked him and, entirely unconvinced, proceeded to cross the street, when a young man who might have been dropped from an aeroplane appeared at my elbow and, lifting his hat, said:

"Right where you are, Madame, for car number ten. Do not cross the street." Before I could answer, the heavenly messenger had disappeared among the passers-by.

Along came a tram marked in big black letters: Stanley Park. But its number was 11, not 10! Would this get me to the park by way of Alaska? I wondered, and decided to take the risk. It would be amusing to telegraph Dan that I was in Nome and would be back for Christmas. Intrigued by the thought I stepped aboard and dropped my seven cents into the fare box; I had made the first move in the game of Going Places Without Sally.

August 13—10:30 A. M.:—On Board S.S. *Princess Marguerite,* bound for Vancouver Island.

Even while I'm watching with amusement the scenes about me on this upper deck, I remember the big basket of flowers sent to me by Mr. C. F. Pratt, which I had, perforce, to leave behind when Dan and I departed from the Hotel Vancouver half an hour ago.

Near me the railing is lined with passengers leaning over, gazing or signalling to friends among the crowd on the shore; men holding pipes or cigars, women holding their hats against the breeze; all of us waiting for the moment when we shall see the steamer move away from the pier. . . . Ropes are cast off. There is a renewed waving of hands and handkerchiefs. Suddenly I see a lad near us, with a little movie camera—no doubt his latest toy—waving the machine wildly up and down as he describes an arc that includes everything from pier to sky. The strip of water widens between ship and shore. Our *Princess Marguerite* speaks, hoarsely for a lady, and, after backing, swings into mid-stream and heads out of Vancouver Harbour.

At once a sense of release seizes the crowd. Everyone becomes active; the ones on deck hurry indoors, and the ones indoors hurry out, with a look of discovery on their faces. Dan and I are caught up in the prevailing mania for being elsewhere, and start along.

Written later:—We roamed around the ship's decks and through its attractive rooms; then returned to this top deck where I settled myself under the protecting

Vancouver Harbour

roof of a space open toward the stern. I hate to be blown about, and I like to be out of doors. After depositing his impedimenta next me on the settee, Dan went off, hair blowing in his eyes, pipe between his teeth, delighted to be on the water.

Gulls are lazily wheeling near the steamer as she goes smoothly forward, making her way through narrowish waters. Along the shores and here and there among the massed green of hill-sides, I see the roofs of cottages. . . . The ship goes steadily forward, moving out into wider water. Toward the right, silhouetted against the sky, lines of a long steel bridge. Brightness is showing between ledges of grey clouds, and far above us shines a patch of blue. . . . A man in my line of vision, sitting on the top of a deck-house, is holding in his arms an enchanting little golden-haired girl. Mother comes along and stands to talk with them a moment, wind blowing her dark hair about her face.

Among the saunterers come two men and a woman— well dressed, foreign, their faces are wide between the cheek bones, the skin thick and white. Seeing empty seats in this protected corner, the three smilingly take possession. The older man makes himself comfortable at the other end of my settee, then, pulling a newspaper out of a pocket of his heavy overcoat, he opens it and points out to his companions a paragraph. As they fix their eyes on the news sheet, I see that it is printed in

Russian. Are they expatriates, refugees, spies? A cloud silently shadows the *Princess Marguerite* and her bright destination. . . .

I must have been asleep. Like the touch of a soft hand on one's forehead is this "wind of the western sea," after Rocky Mountain altitudes. I look around. Gone are the mysterious three. . . . Now here come two big blue-coated creatures. One, as he seats himself at the other end of what I call *my* settee, smiles down upon me like a boy. . . . I smile back at him like a girl, while the man who might be his father, oblivious to this silent exchange of amenities, puts on his spectacles. Then both men open newspapers and settle to the business of learning about the world.

This great blue bear next me is the most intensely masculine creature I have ever encountered. (What would he do, I wonder, if he knew I were writing about himself?) Sometimes, as now, I feel mean, sneaking up on a man with a pencil. This man's large head and regular features have the quality of hewn granite. And such eyelashes! He is looking down now, which gives me a good view of them. They are coarse, and black, and surely the longest eyelashes in the world. Not three feet away from me the man leans forward, arms on knees, great hands holding the wide sheet open to his fixed and downward gaze. Inadvertently I read the newspaper's headline. Can it be? Yes, my dears, what Tarzan is absorbing, motionless and intent, among all the columns of an Australian daily newspaper, is the *Woman's Page!* Silently raising an imaginary glass of prune juice, I drink "To the ladies, God bless 'em!" But, oh, wherefore art thou, Tarzan?

And where the heck is Dan? He has me anchored here with his sun helmet, Stetson hat of Trail Ride days, his overcoat and a dinged heavy camera, not to mention a package of fruit and biscuits. That man Dan drives me crazy when we are on shipboard. He paces round and round the decks with his hair blowing in the wind and a far-off expression on his sun-burned countenance, looking for wonders to happen, looking as though he were expecting prehistoric monsters to rise above the surface of the waters! . . . Well I'll become prehistoric if I wait for him. I shall stagger to the check-room below and get rid of this duffle, and when I meet Dan I'll tell him I've thrown the whole lot overboard. . . .

Later: Relieved of burdens I took a walk about the pleasant interior of the ship. We are now in the midst of the Strait of Georgia—I almost wrote State of Georgia—a flurry of wind and rain has sent many of the passengers indoors. Through the windows of the forward saloon, the water of the Strait looks pea-green, and the far-off mountainous shore a misty purple. Above, blue is still trying to break through the stratified clouds.

Past noon, the ship's siren sounds hoarsely; we are passing slowly through narrows. I ask a lad who is washing paint what this part is called and he replies: "Active passage." That may be a British Columbian joke—I shan't know until I get my hands on a map. For once I seem to be mapless.

The Coffee Room (thanks be, it is not a Shoppee) is the only place where I can round up my wandering Dan. He surely will make his way thither sooner or later. Meanwhile I watch the earnest women, young and less young, who sit at the writing-desks not far away, the lone man and the two little girls—all bending forward, all with heads inclined to the right, and each wearing a conscientious expression on her or his nice healthy face. Health impresses itself on one's attention. I have seen not a person on this boat that looked undernourished. All the children have been quietly happy at their play, showing an extraordinary consideration for the rights of others—quite as much as though they were adults who had been taught by experience. . . .

At last! Dan! He looms in from deck and is arrested in mid-career by the song the orchestra is playing, "Sylvia." He, on one side of the rotunda, listens, and I on the other, entranced as always by the music Oley Speaks wrote for Shakespeare's immortal lyric. The song finished, Dan looks around and, seeing me, grins, then proceeds on his way to the door over which are the magic words "Coffee Room." Having already passed through that door myself, I remain where I now am, happily listening to the orchestra.

The long-dreamed-of island city of Victoria, embowered in trees, is before us as the *Princess Marguerite* draws slowly toward her pier in the harbour of Vancouver Island. From an upper deck of the steamer, Dan and I take in the lovely scene. . . . Now the lines are being thrown to the pier; as we are warped in, I hear the music of bagpipes and see two lads in Scotch tartans who are playing us ashore.

CHAPTER XXVII

AT VICTORIA

TOGETHER with many passengers who had disembarked from the S.S. *Princess Marguerite* at Victoria, Vancouver Island, the Duchess and I left the pier, and walked along beside the Inner Harbour, charmed with the sunlit scene that surrounded us. The island capitol of British Columbia presented an alluring appearance; from the further side of the street on our right hand, wide lawns swept up a rise to handsome grey stone Parliament Buildings whose central dome pointed to a clear blue sky; across the harbour the business section of the city was indicated. At the head of the harbour's sun-lit waters, dominating the picture presented to the sightseer, an imposing pile towered from amidst landscaped grounds; toward it, we, and all our fellow travellers were bending our steps.

"The Empress Hotel!" exclaimed the Duchess. "Do you know, Dan, every traveller from the Pacific Coast that I met in the mountains this summer, sooner or later said to me: 'But wait till you've had tea at the Empress, in Victoria.' Now here we are—and how soft the air is! Think of being at sea level again when only two days ago we were thousands of feet up in the air." With my eye on that famous hotel, and my thought on our bank account, I replied:

"If we're not careful, Duchess, you and I will be up in the air standing right here at the water's edge." But my remark was lost upon her, for at that moment we reached an embowered path leading up to the motor entrance of the hotel and to gardens beyond, of which we had heard. When she turned into this path my hope of getting her established in quarters more in the nature of a tent dissolved into the sweet-scented air.

"We might walk through the gardens," the Duchess suggested, brightly, looking at her watch, "it is a bit early for tea." Inside of me a little voice murmured: "Eventually, so why not now?" I tossed tomorrow over my shoulder, and gave myself up, as the Duchess was doing, to enjoyment of the beauty on every side.

We sauntered along winding paths bordered with luxuriant bloom of countless varieties of plants; through rose gardens that led us to other gardens, and finally to a flower-hedged green lawn shaded with trees, where long chairs invited one to linger.

"Do you think, Dan, we might stretch out for awhile in this blessed sunshine?" asked the Duchess, eyeing, somewhat dubiously, words lettered across the chair backs: "For use of hotel guests only."

"If they try to evict us," I said settling myself with satisfaction in one of the canvas contraptions, with my feet hanging over the end, "I'll simply sign up at the desk; everything seems to point in that direction, anyway, Duchess, so rest your bones."

There was a silent interval during which the beauty of the place sank into me with the sunlight, and then I heard the words:

"This place seems quite near heaven, Dan, although I don't know the length of a spiritual mile."

"We'll soon find out," I replied, getting up; "I'm ready for the celestial equivalent of tea with Devonshire cream and fixings, so, come along," and I pulled the Duchess to her feet. We crossed the rose gardens and took a look at a big building of glass, called the Crystal Garden; in it were tropical plants surrounding a long swimming pool; a badminton court, and a dance floor. Continuing along we found back of the Crystal Garden fine bowling greens where a group of men were playing the ancient game, and spoke of the greens at Sutton Courtney in England where awhile ago we played on turf that has been sacred to bowling since the sixteenth century.

Turning about, the Duchess and I walked back, entering the hotel by way of its conservatory, a bower of mimosa trees, rare plants in bloom, and luxurious green; from its moist and fragrant air we passed into a hand-

Mr. Butchart's Gardens, Victoria

some corridor, getting glimpses each side of a library, drawing rooms, and offices. The lobby led us into the Blue Lounge: a wide high room across the front of the hotel and from which the main entrance gave onto a porch facing the harbour.

Here and there among the chairs and sofas of the lounge small tables set with silver had been placed, and although the time was only three-thirty, pleasant-looking groups of people were already enjoying their afternoon tea. As the Duchess and I seated ourselves in comfortable chairs each side of a little table, she looked around, and smiling with pleasure said:

"One week ago this very day, at this very hour, Dan, you and I after hiking three hours up a mountain had just sat down at a long table out of doors to as good a meal as I ever tasted. It is contrast that gives value, isn't it? And could anything be more of a contrast to the snow-capped peaks of Larch Valley than this charming Victorian scene?"

An hour later, refreshed, we passed through the doorway out onto the broad porch. A rich golden light was over all the scene spread before us. With a gesture of her hand the Duchess indicated the landscaped grounds that led down to the harbour, saying:

"After all, Dan, we're going to be broke anyway, by the time we get home, so why not, for a few dollars extra, decorate the crash with these lovely trees and planting, and all the beauty of Victoria's harbour at sunset?"

"You've got something there, Duchess," I said. "I'll go in and sign the register." And that was the way it came about that while economizing, we spent a week at the Empress Hotel, in Victoria.

CHAPTER XXVIII

SALMON FISHING

I HAD made up my mind that when I got to Vancouver Island I was going to have the fun of catching a salmon on my trout rod; and that if, in doing so, the rod broke into a thousand pieces, well, it would be a glorious finish. The rod must have guessed my thought and, not wishing to end its days in such a fashion, disappeared, because I arrived at one of the world's great salmon fishing centres with nothing but a reel. The Duchess said I was running true to form, and that if ever I should go to Africa to shoot lions, I would arrive there with a fine assortment of ammunition and no rifle.

After reaching Victoria, I soon learned that there are as many ways of catching a salmon as there are of skinning a cat. My education in salmon fishing began as that of thousands before me has begun, by taking what the boatman had to offer in the way of tackle. Then I said my prayers, held my breath and waited for the salmon to strike. But I may as well tell you about it.

Early in the morning of my first day at Victoria I took a West Saanish bus to Brentwood Bay. On arrival

I was disappointed to find Captain Creed already had a boat load of would-be fishers; but when he said, "My son will take you in his boat; he's just as good a fisherman as I and you'll have the boat all to yourself," that seemed good enough. A few minutes later the young man and I chugged away from the dock, with the understanding that he was to put me ashore in time to get the four o'clock bus back to Victoria.

When we were about a quarter of a mile from shore I suddenly realized I had brought no lunch. If the Duchess had been present when I made my hasty departure from the hotel, I should without doubt have been provided with a big basket containing a properly balanced meal. As I ordered my young captain to put into the nearest dock where there would be a store, I could almost hear her saying, "Is it any wonder that at times I am fearful for the future of the human race?"

A few minutes later we came up to a dock and, thinking the boy knew more about the ways of the Island than I did, I handed him a bill, saying, "Get enough for two, and make it snappy." While he was gone to gather food, I examined all the gadgets in the boat. What I saw made me wonder at the way salmon are caught in this part of the world. I had just about made up my mind that by mistake I had got into a boat used for catching whales when my skipper came hurrying down the float toward me. "Heavens!" I thought, seeing the size of the bundle he was carrying, "I must have given him a five dollar bill by mistake." He came aboard, stowed the stuff, started the motor and away we went a second time, out into the bay. Suddenly he turned to me with, "Gosh! I'm sorry, I forgot; here's your change from a dollar," and poured a lot of silver into my hand.

While he rowed along I got the young man to explain things to me, and I learned that salmon grow to be very large, which pleased me tremendously; that they keep themselves as much as 300 feet or more below the surface, and that to reach them a piano wire is used, with a large brass spoon on the business end of it. Weights consisting of old bolts and pieces of iron are attached to the wire about four or five feet above the spoon, in such a way that, when the salmon strikes, a little brass gadget trips, the weights are released, and you have your fish "on the wire," so to speak, with nothing to do but get him alongside, where the Captain, standing ready, gaffs him and hauls him aboard. ("Then," I thought to myself, "the historic event is photographed on a post-card and sent home to Aunt Emma with a few words stating that the fish is on the right!")

We reached a part of the bay where other boats were going along slowly, expectant fishermen holding rods that I well knew they hoped might at any second bend double with the pull of a big salmon. Now my skipper got a line ready; the weights splashed overboard and,

[249]

while the wire was singing as it ran out, he handed me the rod. As I took it into my hands I felt as though I had hooked a kitchen stove. Then the skipper threw over the stern a large peach-basket attached to a rope; this, he explained, was to keep the boat going slowly. Whenever we passed another boat its captain would hold up as many fingers as the number of fish his party had caught, while my captain replied with a negative wave of his hand, back and forth, to show that we were in the red, instead of in the pink.

Charles Dickens will never know how aptly the title of his novel, *Great Expectations,* expressed my mood through that whole blessed day, my first day of fishing for salmon. As time went and brought us no luck, we changed the spoon for a plug. No good; we went back to the spoon. We fished deeper; we fished on the surface. We ate all the lunch, smoked several packs of cigarettes, and, even so, by three o'clock were as free of the smell of fish as though we had been lying on a stack of new-mown hay; yet hope did not fail me, and there were compensations.

A great fish-hawk, that might have been an eagle for all I knew, had established himself in the top of a dead pine tree on the top of a cliff. There in his observation post he was sitting when I discovered him, and man, oh man! did that bird know how to fish! By watching I found that he used the sea gulls as a signal service corps.

There were many schools of small fish in the waters about me. As soon as the gulls caught sight of one of these schools, they would flutter above it, some of them diving to their prey, others landing on the water and swimming madly around, gulping down whatever they could get.

The watcher in the dead pine tree, observing such a scene, would launch out from his high station, ascending in great circles until he was directly over the spot where the gulls were. Then, as they, seeing death was on the wing, flew screeching away, the hawk, like an aeroplane in a power dive with the throttle wide open, would plunge straight down; there would be a spraying of the waters where he struck, a beating of great wings, and the hawk would rise into the air with a fish in his talons. Sometimes the hawk arrived at the spot too late; the fish were gone. He would then sail back to his post on top of the dead pine and wait till the gulls had located another school of unsuspecting fish. And there I sat, representative of a race that has survived this kind of a game through the ages, doing my bit to wipe out the fish. This thought rather took the sting out of not catching any salmon. And then the day itself was so glorious—blue sky above and, reflected in the calm waters of the bay, beautiful forms and shadows of the mountainous shore. It was good merely to be alive.

My skipper proved to be an entertaining companion, he stirred me by stories about fish he and his father had caught, and with tales about life at Brentwood Bay—of fishing carnivals, and sweepstakes held on the Bay on holidays when every boat in the district is out, filled with fishermen who know what is what, and everything is run according to the rules. No boat entered for a prize can start fishing in the morning until the signal has been given, and every boat is obliged to stop at a given time in the evening. Then the catches of the day are weighed, and the prizes, previously exhibited in Victoria by the stores which donate them, are awarded. Thus the hours went by.

I arrived at Brentwood dock just as the four o'clock bus disappeared over the top of the hill, "running true to form," as the Duchess would say. With a two-hour wait ahead of me, I set out to get some refreshment, and found a little shop where I had a cup of coffee and a bite to eat. Thus fortified, I went outdoors again to meditate on the cost of tardiness, but the mood didn't last a minute; there was too much going on.

The Mill Bay-Brentwood Ferry boat had just come in. Cars dashed off it and up the hill as though split seconds of time were of priceless value; other cars raced down the hill to the boat as though in a panic lest the gates would close before they got aboard. Near where I was standing several cars were parked. One, with a New York licence, belonged to a family that were returning from a fishing trip with the captain of their boat, carrying the salmon

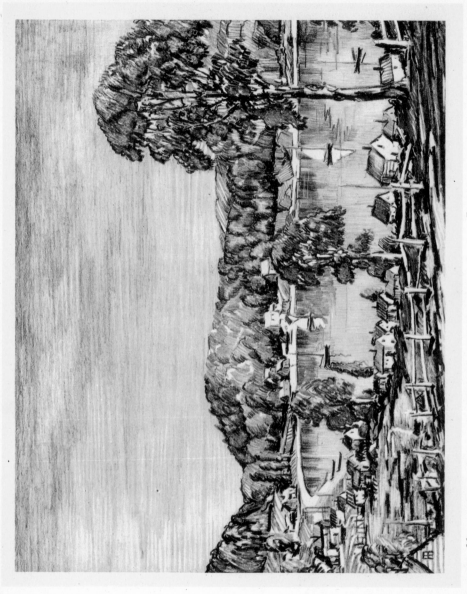

Cadboro Bay, Vancouver Island

they had caught—only one, but quite enough, judging by the excitement of Father, who probably had caught it, of Mother, and of the three children. Placing the salmon on the running-board of the car, the captain received his pay, and, with the thanks of the entire family, departed. Then the fun began. A camera was brought out of the car. Father struck a pose, holding his rod in one hand and the salmon (by the tail) in the other—really a beauty that must have weighed 20 pounds—and Mother snapped a picture. Then the salmon was handed around, and so was the camera, until each one had been taken with the fish, Mother electing to hold the salmon in her arms, with a look of motherhood beaming on her face. The youngest child, not much bigger than the fish itself, dropped the creature in the dust. In a moment the shining thing was covered with mud. If the Star of India had been missed from the British Crown there could not have been more excitement. The little one began to cry. Mother reached into the car, produced a towel, and, with Father holding the fish, she wiped and wiped it with great care, but anyone could see that the glory had departed.

I didn't wait for the end of the play. My bus had arrived, and I jumped aboard, wondering which aunt of the family would receive Father's photograph. "After all," I thought, "perhaps it will be Aunt Emma."

CHAPTER XXIX

MORE SALMON

"Isn't it fun to be setting up housekeeping way out here on the Pacific Coast?" exclaimed the Duchess, as the last piece of our baggage arrived in the living-room of the little cottage we had taken for a month at Oak Bay, about three miles from Victoria.

"Yes," I said, "all due to your discovering while studying a map that we could not go any further west." It was not long before we were settled. Both of us felt the change to sea level.

During the first few days, in taking walks, I discovered, about a mile from our cottage at the southern end of Oak Bay, a boat-house and pier—it wasn't exactly a yacht club—where the people of the neighborhood kept their boats and where skiffs and launches could be hired.

One fine morning the Duchess, having a yen to see more of the shops and stores in Victoria, suggested our taking a trip to town. I declined, as I wanted to make a sketch. Having seen the Duchess into the bus that ran to Victoria from the foot of our street, I wandered off

[254]

looking for something that would keep me busy painting until she returned. My search finally ended at the boathouse, and I walked out onto the end of the pier and sat down. In a moment I was so engrossed with what was going on that all ideas of a sketch evaporated. There was plenty to draw, but I was too interested in watching the scene about me.

It being a fine day, all the young things were out, or getting ready to go out in their one-class boats. Similar to our star class at home, these boats made a great sight as they sailed about the blue waters of the bay.

Below me, tied up to the float at the end of the dock, was an old boat with a small cabin up forward. Out of its rusty stove-pipe curled a wisp of wood smoke. The first whiff sent my mind racing back to Banff, the Trail Ride, and the camp at Larch Valley. Wood smoke always makes me want to go places, always spells some kind of adventure. This old boat must have taken many a beating at sea, from her looks, and I asked a chap next me what kind of a craft it was. He told me that it was used for halibut fishing, far off shore; the owner of it went off alone for days and weeks at a time. As I was looking, the cabin door opened and the owner of this ancient craft came out on deck. He was the counterpart of the boat, looked like a good old Gilbert and Sullivan pirate. He was soon busy coiling his lines in large tubs in the stern. While I was watching the neat way this was

done, a row-doat slid up to the same float and the oc-
cupant threw out an old coat, a lunch basket, and a rod;
then he reached under the seat and, pulling out four big
salmon, threw them one by one onto the float.

When I saw the salmon, something inside of me clicked,
and I dashed up the pier to the boat-house. There I found
the man in charge and asked him, "Can I get a boat to go
fishing?"

"Sure," he said. "How about a rod? Got everything;
fix you up in a moment," and he went on untangling
some tackle that someone like myself had snarled up for
him.

In about fifteen minutes everything was ready, and a
moment later I was afloat in a flat bottom skiff with a
businesslike looking rod of ancient vintage, and with in-
structions to row slowly, go out around the point, then
down another point by the golf club, and, if I got caught
in the tide, to row across it. "Don't try to buck it," said
the man.

With these things to remember I rowed out around the
rocky point that sheltered the little cove where the boat-
house was, hoping that the Duchess's sixth sense would
not be working today; for, if it were, while looking in
a shop window in Victoria, she would see her Dan in a
tiny boat rowing toward the Strait of Juan de Fuca and
the broad Pacific.

What a day it was! Off to the east, rising out of the

blue haze of the coast, I saw the snowy peak of Mount Baker, and to the south, across the Strait in the State of Washington, was the long jagged snow-capped line of the Olympic Range.

When well out along the edge of the kelp, I stopped rowing and was glad to find that the oars were secured in such a way that they could not be lost overboard. Taking up the ancient rod I let out quite a bit of line, braced the rod on the gunnel of my boat, with the butt of it against my foot, and, everything set, started rowing slowly.

There were a number of other fishermen doing the same thing, some with oars like myself; others had a small outboard motor, but none of them I'll wager had set his heart, as mine was, on getting his first salmon.

The tide was ebbing so fast it made rowing easy. As I approached the next point, I saw right on the end of it one of the greens of the Oak Bay Golf Club; the tee was back on some rocks, a drive, I should think, of about two hundred yards.

As I looked, a foursome came onto the tee, and I slowed up my craft to watch them play the hole. The first player's ball landed in a trap, one of the many guarding the green. I could hear the click as the next player hit his ball; he hooked it and I watched it coming, then ping! the ball hit a rock, bounded high in the air, and if my boat had been a yard nearer shore, the ball would have landed in the middle of it. Before I could see what the other players did, the tide, rushing like a mill-race, had whirled me around the point and the tee was lost to sight.

A mile or so ahead I saw an island on which was a lighthouse, and the way the tide was whirling me along it could have been reached in no time, but it meant a long pull back; so I put about and started for the point I had just left. Remembering, however, what the owner of the boat had said, "Don't try to buck the tide," I now rowed off-shore across the tide, then turned back to the point. I had reached the point and was just on the edge of the kelp when suddenly the tip of my pole took a dive and the reel began to sing. I dropped the oars, grabbed the rod and gave a mighty heave, to find that there was a fish on the line; it went off like a race horse.

My heart now sounded to me like a machine-gun. Then, oh, then, he came out of water in a great leap, a big silvery salmon; I had caught my first salmon, all by myself. The next thing to do was not to lose him. Down he went, then up, in a series of jumps, I holding on, and reeling like mad to get him up to the boat. Suddenly I realized that I had no net. The salmon was in close now, and, as if knowing his danger, he came out of the water in a beautiful jump, trying to shake out the hook.

As I brought the fish alongside I was so excited I

[258]

wouldn't have been surprised to see my heart hopping around in the bottom of the boat. A little prayer went up as, with a mighty heave, I landed my fish. He was minded not to stay but, with a pair of number 12 shoes, and two large hands, and 200 pounds to back them up, I convinced the fish that it was all over but the shouting; and shout I did with joy of conquest. It was not a great fish, weighing I should think about 15 pounds.

I stuffed the salmon under the back seat, guarding him with both feet, and started rowing for home. I had had enough excitement, and besides I just could not wait to show my prize to the Duchess.

Keeping out of the tide, and close to shore, I was back at the dock in no time, paying for my boat. With the salmon well wrapped in paper, I set off for the cottage.

As I went up the steps of the porch, the Duchess came out of the living-room.

"Where have you been?" she asked.

"Walking," I replied. And then, even as Cleopatra was unrolled from a carpet in front of Caesar, I unrolled from its paper my silvery Cohoe.

"What a beauty!" exclaimed the Duchess. "Where did you buy it?"

"Buy it?" I shouted. "I caught it!" And we had an appropriate celebration.

After this first adventure, I made various fishing trips

at Oak Bay Harbour—one in particular, with Mr. Montieth of Victoria, who showed me how to catch salmon with a light rod and a Bucktail fly. This was the grandest fun of all.

CHAPTER XXX

LOOKING HOMEWARD

The Duchess's Diary

Oak Bay, Vancouver Island. August 28:—As I place this diary on one of three tables set against as many open windows of a little tea room on the pier at Oak Bay, the rich colours of a Royal Doulton tea pot, cups and saucers, are still delighting my eyes. Dan, fortified with toasted raisin buns, and several cups of the brew that cheers, has gone out to fraternize with fishermen at the end of the pier where he will get the latest news of salmon. With great content I remain here, looking out upon a curving sandy beach where happy children play beside blue water, under an azure sky.

A real estate agent of a kind made especially in Vancouver Island (he took pains to be helpful *after* he had signed us up for a lease, as well as before) was the means of our finding an attractive care-free cottage with a garden and the use of a car, near the shore in this charming suburb of Victoria. The owner of the cottage, an English woman with a sense of humour and knowledge of Vancouver Island has done a great deal to make our sojourn enjoyable; her little black dog by taking us on, and dropping in for an hour with us now and then makes us feel established, and very much at home.

There are good markets near at hand in Oak Bay, so I am beginning to learn somewhat of the place; marketing is the best way of getting Current Events and Local History wrapped and tucked into a basket. And as for shopping in Victoria's fascinating stores—it should be listed among the sports to be enjoyed, along with tennis and golf.

Dan and I came to Victoria intending to stay four days, we've been here weeks. Since we came I've heard many stories of persons who visited Victoria out of curiosity, and remained for the rest of their lives. That isn't hard to understand, what with peace, a temperature never below forty-two nor above seventy-one degrees; fishing, and golf, and beautiful gardens; colonies of pleasant, intelligent, leisured people; and excellent steamers to bring the great world into Victoria's harbour, and to take it away again before it can do any harm.

Mr. Cash, in charge of the enforcement of game laws on Vancouver Island together with his wife Gwen Cash, a writer, took us on a long ride late one afternoon and evening to show us places of particular interest, ending at the Chalet at Deep Cove. The cove itself is beautiful; we sat looking out upon its waters and its wooded shores in the after-glow of sunset while dinner was prepared for us. The dinner was excellent and by the time we were leaving to drive back to Victoria Dan and I both felt we would like to return to the Chalet sometime for a sojourn. On the drive home I learned that it was an uncle of Mr. Cash who established the first experimental farm in Vancouver Island.

We have motored to many places of interest: to the Observatory, with its great astro-physical telescope; to the gardens of Mr. and Mrs. Butchart, sixteen beautiful acres of them; we have seen the famous Malahat Drive and stopped for tea at Malahat Lookout where we enjoyed a marvellous view; and we have been to Beacon Hill Park, seen its famous Garry Oaks, enjoyed the Marine Drive. But not yet have we been "up-island," as the expression is here; and everyone knows that the Forbidden Plateau, and the fishing at Campbell River are things to be seen and experienced.

Why should one ever leave Vancouver Island?

September 1. 10:45 A. M. From a headland of the eastern shore of Vancouver Island, at Oak Bay this first day of September, I look across the Strait of Georgia to the invisible Washington shore of the United States;

along that eastern horizon, shadowy against a pale sky, rise the Olympics. Mount Baker's snowy head, so often visible is nowhere to be seen. Air, that has the quality of silk, stirs the grasses near me and a sheen, as of silk, is over all the scene.

Below, at water level, jagged rocks rise out of the sands, and from them a beach begins and sweeps south in a crescent that is reaped by a scimitar of steel-blue water, smooth as a blade.

Below me in a cove, among grey rocks, two little boys in bathing-suits play with their dog; they gather armfuls of coarse green kelp at water's edge, and pile it above water line, only to leave it and run with their dog along the hard wet sand. Red roofs and green roofs of cottages show among trees all the way to the southern horn of the crescent beach.

The wide blue sky overhead is wiped clean, save for a long faint sigh of cirrus cloud near the Strait of Juan de Fuca.

11:45 A. M. All the blue surface of the bay, from shore to the dark green islands of San Juan, Orcas, Lopez, and as far as one can see, is broken into lapping wavelets whose dancing crests catch the sun and toss it into a million flashing jewels of light. Three little boats with single white sails, skim like birds around and between the islands.

Now there comes to me, high on the cliff as I gaze beyond Ten Mile Point, a steady push of fresher air from the Strait of Georgia, with a smell of the open sea.

On the 28th of September, Sally, with her head up, went trotting through swanky Lenox, Massachussetts; we had bought her a new bonnet when we took her out of storage in Montreal, and she was showing her pleasure by stepping out.

"Now that we are down to sea level again, Duchess," I remarked, "and likely to remain there for some time, what are you going to do with your riding boots?"

"Because of what they have done to me," she exclaimed, "I feel sure they are more than inanimate matter. Think, Dan, of all the adventures that have befallen us since the June day in our attic when I found those old California boots in a trunk. The minute they were on my feet they made off, I dragging you after me, over plains and rivers, across lakes, through valleys and up mountains till we both had to sit down on the backbone of the continent to catch our breath. They yanked me up altitudes and let me down again till I felt like a sliding trombone; made me parade over rocky peaks and dance the Suzie Q. on ice of age-old glaciers. Why, my dear,"—the Duchess was laughing so that a man beside the road smiled in response as we whirled past him, "what those boots haven't done to me is too little to be mentioned."

"The way you put it, Duchess," I said, "makes it seem that they are Boots with a capital."

"That's it—you've got it!" cried the Duchess excitedly: "capital, capitol, Washington, D.C., Smithsonian Institution. I shall write to the secretary as soon as I reach home and announce a bequest of a pair of famous boots."

"If you do, Duchess," I was laughing with her as we rode on through the blessed New England countryside, "be sure to mention the fact that the boots are shod with starry Hungarian hobnails."

Finis

RAILROAD MILEAGE, TIME AND STATIONS

THE DOMINION

MILES	STATIONS	TIME OF DEPARTURE		DAYS
0	Montreal 7:50	Eastern Standard	P. M.	
111	Ottawa 10:10	" "	P. M.	
437	Sudbury 6:20	" "	A. M.	First
991	Fort William . 9:55	Central Time	P. M.	
1,410	Winnipeg 10:15	" "	A. M.	Second
1,674	Broad View .. 4:20	Mountain Time	P. M.	
1,766	Regina 6:50	" "	P. M.	
1,808	Moose Jaw ... 8:20	" "	P. M.	
1,918	Swift Current .11:15	" "	P. M.	
2,066	Medicine Hat . 3:40	" "	A. M.	Third
2,242	Calgary ..... 9:00 Arrive	" "	A. M.	
2,323	Banff 12:00	" "	M.	

THE MOUNTAINEER

MILES	STATIONS	TIME OF DEPARTURE		DAYS
2,358	Lake Louise ..11:00	Mountain Time	A. M.	
2,378	Field 11:40	Pacific Time	A. M.	
2,413	Golden 1:07	" "	P. M.	
2,464	Glacier 3:25	" "	P. M.	
2,483	Albert Canyon 4:28	" "	P. M.	
2,504	Revelstoke ... 5:20	" "	P. M.	
2,549	Sicamous 7:00	" "	P. M.	
2,633	Kamloops 10:20	" "	P. M.	
2,754	North Bend .. 3:10	" "	A. M.	Fourth
2,883	Vancouver ... 7:45 Arrive	" "	A. M.	

TEN SUPERB RIVERS SEEN ON TRIP

CALGARY—VANCOUVER

The Bow River	at	Calgary, Alta.—Altitude		3,438
The Kicking Horse River	"	Hector, B.C.	"	5,219
The Columbia River	"	Golden, B.C.	"	2,583
The Beaver River	"	Beavermouth, Alta.	"	2,433
The Illecillewaet River	"	Glacier, B.C.	"	3,778
The Tonkawatla River	"	Revelstoke, B.C.	"	1,494
The Eagle River	"	Craigellachie, B.C.	"	1,224
The Thompson River	"	Kamloops, B.C.	"	1,159
The Fraser River	"	Lytton, B.C.	"	693
		and runs to		
		within 24 miles		
		of Vancouver	"	14

INDIANS OF ALBERTA AND BRITISH COLUMBIA

The Assiniboine, or Stony Indians: Of the foot-hills. About 1,400 in Canada. Mountain tribe proverbially reliable, truthful, generous. Peace-loving. Reservation: Morley, Alberta. Noted for bead work.

The Athapascan Nation:.......
Sarcee
Beaver
Carrier
Sehanais

Their language widely distributed—Alaska to New Mexico.

The Blackfoot Nation:.........
Belong to the Algonkin. Largest Reservation at Gleichen, east of Calgary. Some of them prosperous and wealthy.

Blood—Reservation at Macleod,
largest in Canada
Piegan—Reservation at Brocket

[268]

SUPPLEMENT

The Cree Nation: . . . .
                    Plains Cree
                    Swampy Cree
                    Western Cree
The Kootenay Nation: . . . . On four reserves. Headquarters,
                              Steele, B.C. Mountain Indians.
The Salish Nation: . . . . Since ancient times in S.E. Brit-
                              ish Columbia.
                    The Shuswap (largest Salish
                       tribe)
                    The Thompson River Indians
                    The Ikanagan River Indians
                    The Coast Salish . Flatten the head to show culture.

A BOUQUET OF ALPINE FLOWERS

Gathered along trails in the Canadian Rockies

July 10 to August 10

Arnica, Alpine; Heart-leaved
Asters, Engelmann's; Fremont's

Beard-tongue, Large Purple
Bunchberry

Campion, Moss; White
Capberry
Chalice Cup, the decorative seed pods only
Cinquefoil, Shrubby
Columbine, Western; Yellow

Dogwood, Red Oskier; called by Western Indians, Kinnikinic
Dryas, Drummond's

Erigonum, tall
Everlasting, Mouse-ear; Silky; Tall; White

[269]

Fleabane, Large Purple; Rough
Fly Honeysuckle
Forget-me-not, Mountain

Gaillardia, Black-eyed Susan
Gentian, Northern
Geranium, White

Harebell, Arctic
Hawkweed, Hairy
Heath, White
Heather, White Mountain; Red
Heliotrope, Northern

Labrador Tea, Woolly
Ladies' Tresses, Hooded
Larkspur, Blue-veined

Orchis, Long-bracted Rein; White Rein

Paint Brush, Lance-leaved; Red Indian; White Indian
Pasque Flower, seed head only, like feathery tufts
Phacelia, Mountain

Queen Cup, *Clintonia Uniflora*

Ragwort, Silvery Groundsel

Saxifrage, Alpine; Yellow; Tall
Silverweed
Speedwell, Alpine; Yellow
Spiraea, Birch-leaved
Stitchwort, Long-stalked

Twinflower, Northern

Vetch, Slender Milk; Macoun's Milk

Wintergreen, One-flowered; Green-flowered; One-sided

Yarrow

TREES OF THE CANADIAN ROCKIES

White-Bark Pine:

Evergreen tree 20–50 feet high, found at altitudes 5,000–7,000 feet. Distinguished by creamy-white plate-like scales of bark; branches flexible and stout; cones purplish-brown, no stems, grow at end of branch. The large sweet seeds are eaten by Indians. In highest altitudes, tree becomes prostrate.

Mountain Pine:

A tree 50–100 feet high, slender; branches slightly drooping; bark pale grey on young trees; bark of mature tree divided into square plates having flat purple scales. Leaves deep blue-green covered with bloom; cones long, hanging, thicker and smoother toward their tops, terminating in prickly protuberance.

Bull Pine:

150–200 feet high. Stem massive; branches thick, much forked; often turned up at end. Bark cinnamon-red, brown or nearly black, broken in ridges with appressed scales. Leaves dark yellow-green, marked by stomata on the three faces, are five to eight inches long.

Lodge Pole Pine:

Often called Jack or Black pine. Small, slender tree; branches horizontal below turn upward to a pyramidal top. Bark light orange-brown, a distinguishing characteristic. Leaves light green; cones small, oval, shining, yellowish-brown. Abundant in mountains.

Lyall's Larch:

Small, charming tree, not evergreen. Seen often above the last of the trees at snow line, where it has but three months of growing weather, and nine in which to endure Arctic winds and temperatures. Leaves pale green, grow in cluster out of woody cups on short lateral branches, turn completely yellow in September before they fall. Cones small, soon drop off. Many of these lovely larches are to be seen in Larch Valley above Moraine Lake, where in 1937 the Sky Line Trail Hikers encamped.

White Spruce:

Has a graceful form, pyramidal in outline; needles are sharp, pointed and crowded; light blue-green or bluish; cones oblong and pendulous; foliage has unpleasant smell.

Englemann Spruce:

Evergreen. 50–150 feet high; sometimes 5 feet in diameter. Grows where altitude is between 5,000 and 7,000 feet. Widely distributed. Bark rich cinnamon colour; leaves sharp, and blue-green, harsh to the touch. Cones droop. This tree has a disagreeable smell.

Balsam Fir:

Evergreen. 50–75 feet high. Small conifer, bark smooth, with shallow fissures, cinnamon-red scales. Lower branches droop; upper branches form spire-like head. Foliage feels soft. Needles whitish below, with a green mid rib, and two resin-ducts. Buds are small, round and gummy. Fragrant.

Western Hemlock:

Tall evergreen, feathery in appearance, with small cones. Bark reddish-brown; leaves strongly grooved, lustrous on top, white below.

Mountain Hemlock:

Large evergreen; leaves bright green above and below standing out from all sides of branches. Cones erect when young, drooping at maturity.

Douglas Fir:

Grows 100 to 300 feet high and from 2 to 15 feet in diameter. Glossy crowded leaves, yellow-green on top with green midnerve beneath; trunk covered with rough brown bark rises straight as a mast. Cones are pendant on long strong stems and have trident shaped bracts below their scales. Help to save these glorious trees from the axe of the lumberman!

Red Cedar:

A most lovely tree! Grows to 250 feet; foliage evergreen, shining, with a general effect of laciness; branches drooping. Bark thin and bright cinnamon red, broken on surface into strips. Cones cinnamon color, thickly clustered at the ends of bracts.

Rocky Mountain Juniper:

Grows 10–50 feet high. Berry-like cones are bright blue, sweet, and covered with whitish bloom. There is a creeping variety about three feet high.

Alpine Juniper:
Is almost prostrate. Grows in circular patches sometimes 10 feet in diameter. Found at extremely high altitudes, at last growth of tree line. Berries round, smooth, and dark blue. Leaves sometimes whitened on surface.

Aspen Poplar:
Slender tree; thin yellowish-brown or pale bark. Heart-shaped leaves on slender stems, tremble. Flower-like catkins. Its light-green delicate foliage a welcome sight among dark spruce of the mountains.

Western Balsam Poplar:
Bark smooth, ash-grey. Branches stout, upright, and spreading. Large buds, fragrant and resinous. Leaves egg shape, on long stems, and finely toothed; dark green on top, pale underneath. Catkins slender.

Cottonwood:
Smaller than the Balsam Poplar; branches stout and spreading, ascend, forming a rounded head. Leaves very pointed, toothed except near base and tip. Bark pale grey, stems in young trees smooth and nearly white.

Black Birch:
Small tree, bark smooth, a lustrous copper or bronze. Leaves pale-green above, yellowish beneath, in autumn turn completely yellow.

Western Mountain Ash:
The Rowan tree of song and story. Usual growth 6–15 feet. Leaves dark green on top, pale underneath. Flowers, pale coloured in clustered cymes, of a pungent odour. Berries, bright red, give the tree, together with its foliage of decorative character, a striking appearance.

ALBERTA

CUSTOMS REGULATIONS

Tourists entering Canada do not require passports. Automobiles may be brought into Canada for purpose of health or pleasure for a period up to 90 days without duty or bond, and for a period up to six months by fulfilling certain security requirements. It is absolutely unnecessary for a tourist entering Canada to pay any fee for an automobile entry permit or its extension, as Canadian Customs Officers will, without charge, assist the tourist in making out all forms.

For Twenty-four Hours. Automobiles may be entered at any Canadian port for touring purposes for a period not exceeding 24 hours, by the owner surrendering his State license card, which is handed to him on his return journey.

For Two to Sixty Days. For a period of sixty days a motorist may bring his car into Canada for touring purposes only and return by a port of entry or any other port without bond or deposit, the only requirements being the possession of a State licence identifying the car, and the completion of the necessary duplicate customs form, on which particulars of the car are recorded. One form is retained by the Customs Officer and one by the motorist, which is to be surrendered by him at any port of exit on leaving Canada.

For Sixty to Ninety Days. One extension of thirty days to a limit of ninety may be granted without a bond or deposit by presenting the original customs permit to any Customs Officer.

For One to Six Months. Automobiles may be entered at Canadian port of Customs for touring purposes, for a period of one to six months, by filling in the same form referred to, and signing a bond in approved form for double the amount of the estimated duties on the vehicle, or secure a special bond of an incorporated guarantee company authorized to do business in Canada.

The automobile of any tourist not returning within the time limit is liable to seizure. Should an unforeseen delay occur, prolonging the time of stay in Canada beyond that mentioned in the tourist's permit, the Customs Department, Ottawa, should be communicated with at once.

For information regarding the admission of Motor Cycles, Bicycles, Pleasure Boats, Tourists' Outfits, Travellers' Baggage, Dogs and Pets, etc., please apply to the Customs Department, Ottawa, or nearest Canadian Customs Officer.

Ports of Entry—From the United States into Alberta—Aden,

Cardston, Carway, Coutts, Twin Lakes, Waterton Lakes, Wild Horse.

From Alberta into the United States—Gateway, Roosville, Peigean, Peskan, Sweet Grass, Havre.

REGISTRATION OF CARS

Motorists entering Alberta from the United States for a period not exceeding six months, are not required to register their cars with the police, but must at all times be prepared to produce their port of entry customs permit when required to do so by members of the police.

Motorists from other provinces in Canada, entering Alberta, must within 24 hours of their arrival, register their machines with the police, and obtain therefrom a certificate of registration, with which will be furnished a wind-shield sticker which will be evidence of registration.

A non-resident chauffeur who has complied with the laws of his own place of residence as to licensing of chauffeurs need not be licensed in Alberta while driving the vehicle of a non-resident exempt from registration.

AUTO CAMPS

The following camps, located at the under-mentioned places, are equipped with a supply of wood, stove and cook-house equipment, which reaches greater pretensions in the larger centres.

On Highway No. 1 (Going North)—Cardston, Macleod, Claresholm, Nanton, Okotoks, Calgary, Crossfield, Carstairs, Didsbury, Bowden, Innisfail, Red Deer, Lacombe, Ponoka, Wetaskiwin, Millet, Edmonton, Athabasca, Slave Lake, Faust, Peace River.

On Highway No. 2 (Going West)—Medicine Hat, Bassano, Calgary, Banff (Castle Mountain, etc.), Lake Louise.

On Highway No. 3 (Going South-west)—Medicine Hat, Lethbridge, Macleod, Pincher Creek, Blairmore, Coleman.

On Highway No. 4—Lethbridge.

On Highway No. 9 (Going North-east)—Drumheller, Hanna.

On Highway No. 11—Sylvan Lake.

On Highway No. 12 (Going South-east) —Lacombe, Stettler, Castor, Coronation.

On Highway No. 13 (Going East and South-east) —Camrose, Hardisty, Provost.

On Highway No. 14 (Going South-east) —Edmonton, Tofield, Holden, Viking, Wainwright, Chauvin.

On Highway No. 16 (Going West) —Lloydminster, Vermilion, Innisfree, Vegreville, Fort Saskatchewan, Edmonton, Seba Beach, Edson, Jasper Park.

On Highway No. 20 (Going West) —Lacombe, Gull Lake.

On Highway No. 23 —Barons.

On Highways in B.C., adjacent to Alberta—Lake Windermere, Kootenay.

On Highways in Montana, adjacent to Alberta—Glacier Park.

A small fee is charged at the larger camps.

BUNGALOW CAMPS

Bungalow Camps provide moderately-priced accommodations for tourists at attractive scenic points in the Canadian Rockies and elsewhere. These consist of small living and sleeping bungalows clustered around a larger building containing kitchen, dining and lounging rooms, the latter with an open fireplace. All the buildings are one story, of rustic design, and of frame or log construction. Each of the camps has been located so as to make accessible Alpine districts of exceptional beauty. While the meals are good and substantial, and the beds most comfortable, the rates are very moderate. These camps are less formal than the large resort hotel, and very much favoured by people who prefer to be where there is a quiet and informal atmosphere, and where sport or old clothes can be worn at all times; also contains bathrooms, and a good lighting system.

The principal bungalow camps of Alberta are to be found in the Rockies at Castle Mountain, Moraine Lake, Mount Assiniboine, and other mountain resorts.

TEA HOUSES

Tea houses in the Rockies are comfortably furnished buildings with covered verandas, built for the accommodation of trail hikers or riders to relax for short periods while on the trail, and obtain meals and lighter lunches. They are located at suitable hiking distances from the resort hotels and bungalow camps, and at vantage points of unusual interest and beauty.

ALPINE HUTS

Alpine Huts are erected in the Rockies for the accommodation and convenience of mountaineers. Huts are furnished with cots, bedding, stove, firewood, kitchen utensils, etc., but have no one in charge.

MOTOR ROADS

Calgary to Banff	85.	Miles
Banff to Castle	19.9	"
Castle to Lake Louise	22.	"
Lake Louise to Field	16.	"
Field to Switchback	8.	"
Field to Takakaw Falls	11.	"
Field to Emerald Lake	7.	"
Field to Golden	38.	"
Banff-Windemere Highway: Firlands, B.C. to Castle, Alberta	72.	"
Columbia River Road: Firlands, B.C. to Golden	67.	"

A motor bus service is maintained by the C.P.R. between Banff and Golden. Stopover privileges are given to rail passengers who may wish to take advantage of the opportunity to see by motor the scenic wonders of this section of the Canadian Rockies.

The new Kicking Horse motor road used for the Motor Detour mentioned above, winds along for miles above the level of the railway.

NATIONAL PARKS

Banff Park	2,585.0	square miles
Buffalo Park	197.5	" "

Elk Island Park .... 51.0 " "
Jasper Park .... 4,200.0 " "
Nemiskam Park .... 8.5 " "
Waterton Lakes Park .... 220.0 " "
Wawaskesy Park .... 54.0 " "

The parks are administered by the Department of the Interior at Ottawa, through the National Parks of Canada Service. The local administration is in the hands of superintendents whose offices are located at convenient and important points in these parks. The superintendent of the Banff National Park has his office in the Administration building, which is situated on Banff Avenue, Banff, at the north end of the Bow bridge. Kootenay National Park headquarters are situated at Radium Hot Springs, in the building which forms the entrance gateway to the park. The superintendent of Yoho National Park has his offices in the park headquarters building which is located at the railway station, Field, B.C. Visitors to the park may make inquiry at any one of these three offices for any information required, and may also apply at the Information Bureau at Banff, situated immediately adjacent to the Administration building. Gatekeepers at the three entrance gates, Banff, Radium Hot Springs (Kootenay), and Leanchoil (Yoho), will also furnish information and answer inquiries whenever possible. Copies of Parks' and Motor Regulations and literature dealing generally with the parks may be had free of charge on application.

Transient licences are issued to motorists entering Banff, Kootenay and Yoho Parks. A fee of two dollars is charged, which entitles the holder to motor in any or all of these parks and also gives him free camping privileges on any recognized campground in the National parks during the thirty days immediately following the date of issue of the licence.

No hunting is permitted within the parks and all firearms must be sealed upon entry. Guns will be sealed free of charge at the Superintendents' offices or by any of the park wardens. Wild birds, their nests and eggs are rigidly protected.

Visitors to the parks should not undertake trail or climbing expeditions without competent guides and equipment. Experienced outfitters and licensed guides are located at various points in the park.

Visitors are warned against feeding bears or placing food for them at camps.

Be careful with fire. Visitors are expected to use the camping grounds provided at convenient points. These camps are maintained for the benefit and convenience of visitors and are equipped with stoves, tables, etc.

Keep camps clean. Leave them clean. Burn or bury all refuse promptly—even tin cans—to prevent flies and to get them out of sight.

Build your campfire on dirt. Scrape around it, removing all inflammable material within a radius of from 3 to 5 feet. Put your fire out. In ten minutes go back and put it out again. Never build a campfire against a tree or log, in leaf mould or rotten wood. Build all fires away from overhanging branches.

Hundreds of fires escape each year after campers have thought they were extinguished. It is advisable to soak thoroughly all embers and charred pieces of wood and then cover them with dirt. Feel around the outer edge of the fire pit to make sure no fire is smouldering in charred roots or leaf mould.

Break your match in two before you throw it away. Make it a habit. Drop pipe, cigar or cigarette ashes only on dirt. Then stamp them out.

Never break bottles (glass is dangerous) or leave them where the sun may focus through them and start fire.

Never defile water.

Do not bark or chip trees needlessly, or drive nails in them.

Protect the wild flowers. Don't pull them up by the roots. Don't pick many of them and particularly along roadsides where they can be enjoyed by all. Don't take the rare kinds at all. Help to preserve them for future years. Help to keep the parks beautiful.

Should you discover a forest fire report it immediately to the chief warden or the nearest Park official.

PEAKS ENCIRCLING LAKE LOUISE

	Altitude
Saddleback Mountain	7,993
Fairview Mountain	9,011
Sheol Mountain	9,118
Aberdeen Mountain	10,350
Mount Lefroy	11,230
Victoria Mountain	11,365
Whyte Mountain	9,786
Big Beehive Mountain	7,440
Niblock	9,764
St. Piran	8,691
Little Beehive Mountain	7,100

HUNTING IN ALBERTA

BIG GAME

Big Horned Sheep is the most sought after trophy, and is found in various localities, from the Waterton Lakes Park in the south to within one hundred miles of Peace River, in the north.

Mountain Goat has a wider range, and though the old billies choose their homes in the more rugged mountains, they are found in most sections of the mountains throughout the length of the province.

Woodland Caribou and sub species, called Osborne Caribou, have their range from the Athabasca River north along the foothills, and in the mountains to the British Columbia boundary.

Elk have had a closed season for a number of years, and were mostly found in the Pembina-Brazeau Elk Reserve. As their numbers increased they spread to adjacent areas. As these are gregarious animals it was found advisable to open the season for a limited number of licences which permits only the older bulls with heads of ten points and over to be taken.

Mule Deer. These large-eared species of the deer family are found in the foothills and mountains, from the Waterton Lakes Park to the northern part of the Province. These provide very attractive hunting for the sportsmen who can afford time and expenses for short trips only.

Moose also provides excellent hunting north of the Calgary-Banff branch of the C.P.R. Railroad to the northern part of the province. In the more remote areas they are quite plentiful, and good trophies may be secured.

Grizzly and Black Bear always provide a thrill for the hunter and in the fall are found in the most unsuspected places. They cover a wide range of hunting area, and are very difficult to hunt in the fall of the year, when they feed mostly on roots and berries in the timber and park areas. To ensure reasonable success in bear hunting, sportsmen should plan their hunts in the spring when the bear come out in the green slides for their earliest food supplies.

Reliable outfitters and guides who are licensed under proper recommendations and credentials, may be secured in any locality that affords good hunting.

BIRD GAME

The Duck Season is open from September 15 to November 15, and improved travelling conditions now provide an incentive to sportsmen to go further afield for the splendid sport of duck hunting. The limit for a day's shoot is fifteen before October 1, and twenty-five per day thereafter, with a limit for the season of one hundred.

Sunday shooting, and the use of live decoys, is prohibited.

Most of the up-land game birds have a cycle which is coincident with the supply of rabbits. It is expected that for the next two or three years Sharp-tailed Grouse, commonly called Prairie Chicken, Ruffed Grouse, Spruce Grouse, and Ptarmigan, will be in fair supply in the localities to which they are adapted. If the spring hatching season is unfavourable, the bag limits must necessarily be reduced to coincide with the supply.

The European Grey Partridge, commonly called Hungarian Partridge, was introduced into Alberta by prominent sportsmen, over twenty years ago, and they increased in such numbers as to provide excellent sport. The season which opens on October 1 and extends

[281]

for two months, gives bird hunters excellent opportunity for real sport.

To appreciate Hungarian Partridge shooting, at its best, hunters should provide themselves with bird dogs, as these Partridges, when wounded, are very difficult to retrieve. The use of sporting dogs for any bird game shooting adds greatly to the pleasure, as hunters must necessarily lose a proportion of the wounded birds unless a trained dog is available for retrieving.

The Chinese and Mongolian Pheasant have been released from time to time, and have shown satisfactory increase in most districts. There is a continuous closed season on these birds.

Information regarding game regulations and licences may be obtained from the Game Commissioner, Department of Agriculture, Edmonton, Canada. Copies of the game regulations, with the various hunting seasons, will be sent on application. Alberta has also a Fish and Game Protective Association, with several branches in different centres of the Province.

NON-RESIDENT FEES

Outfitter's Licence	$50.00
General Game Licence	50.00
Permit to hunt Bear on Forest Reserve	25.00
Game Bird Licence (issued to resident of Canada outside of Alberta)	10.00
Game Bird Licence (issued to non-resident of Canada, except under special permit)	25.00
Special Big Game Licence	50.00
Special Elk Licence	50.00
Guest Game Bird Licence, per day	5.00

FISHING IN ALBERTA

The best fishing in the province is to be found in the mountain streams of the Rocky Mountains and foothills, in the semi-wooded and wooded areas of the north and in the Laurentian country.

The following brief description of most of the best fishing localities may serve as a guide to those seeking this kind of sport.

SUPPLEMENT

Waterton Lakes Park—Fairly good lake trout fishing may be secured in the main, Crow's Nest road or side roads branching off this road at Pincher, Cowly tributary streams. In Cameron Lake rainbow and speckled trout, recently introduced, are doing well and increasing yearly. Good fishing is now obtained in that lake. In the north lake pike are plentiful and of good size. These are accessible by motor road.

Tributaries of Kootenay River—In Drywood River and Yarrow Creek, cutthroat and rainbow trout and Rocky Mountain whitefish are the chief species caught. Accessible by motor from Pincher to Waterton Park.

Belly River—Rocky Mountain whitefish and a few Dolly Varden trout. Accessible by motor road from Waterton to Cardston and Hillspring to Cardston.

St. Mary's River—There is fair fishing at Kimbal, southeast of Cardston at the head-gates of the Canadian Pacific Railway irrigation. The chief species are cutthroat trout, Rocky Mountain whitefish and Dolly Varden trout. Accessible by motor road about twelve miles from Cardston.

Tributaries of the Old Man River—Pincher Creek, South Fork, Crow's Nest River and Lakes, and the main stream of the Old Man River into the Crow's Nest forest reserve with upper tributaries that are open, Livingstone, Carbondale and Castle rivers, West Branch of Castle River and that portion of Race Horse Creek from the mouth of Daisy Creek eastward. In these streams are cutthroat trout, Dolly Varden trout, Rocky Mountain whitefish and some rainbow trout which have been introduced within recent years. All reached by motor roads either main, Crow's Nest road or side roads branching off this road at Pincher Creek, or Lundbreck.

East of Lethbridge—Good pike fishing in Chin Lakes. There is no accommodation except at Lethbridge and Taber. There is a good motor road to the lake.

West of Nanton—There is good fishing in the north and south branches of Willow Creek (all tributaries of these streams closed) chiefly cutthroat and rainbow trout and Rocky Mountain whitefish. It is necessary to go about thirty miles west. The road is good in dry weather.

[283]

West of High River—In the Highwood River only the main stream is open within and without the forest reserve. All tributaries are closed. The trout fishing is excellent with cutthroat and rainbow trout, and also some Rocky Mountain whitefish and Dolly Varden trout. The best fishing is about thirty-five miles west, the road is good from High River. Accommodation may be had at a number of ranches in the vicinity and also at High River, while Calgary is only forty miles from High River with well surfaced road.

West of Okotoks—The north and south branches of Sheep Creek and also Fisher Creek are open outside the Forest reserves, but closed within. Fishing improves on approaching the forest reserve. There is a good road to Lineham and also to Kew, but above these points travel is merely by trails, occasionally by car. This fishing locality can be reached by automobile either by way of Okotoks or direct from Calgary by way of Priddis or Millarville.

West of Calgary: Elbow River—Cutthroat and Dolly Varden trout on the upper reaches. Lower down the river is too large for good fishing, accessible by motor. This river is also open in the forest reserve, all tributaries are closed within and without the forest reserve. The Bow River has good fishing west of Cochrane on the main stream. To catch fish here requires expert angling but excellent catches have been taken of cutthroat and rainbow trout. Some fine catches have also been taken east of Cochrane. The Jumping Pond is also a good trout stream but is fished very heavily—principally cutthroat trout and some rainbow trout.

Banff Park—All waters within reach of motor highways in the park are heavily fished, but excellent fishing (cutthroat and Dolly Varden) can be obtained at Spray Lakes and Kananaskis Lakes, both of which can be reached by packhorse and saddle horse. Spray Lakes are twenty miles from Canmore and thirty miles from Banff. Kananaskis Lakes are forty-five miles from Canmore. These lakes can also be reached from Seebe or Morley. Guides can be secured at Banff, Canmore or Seebe. There is also good salmon trout fishing in Lake Minnewanka, eight miles from Banff by a good motor road. Boats are available here.

In the Bow and Spray Rivers, Dolly Varden and cutthroat trout and Rocky Mountain whitefish provide good fishing. There is also

[284]

good fishing at Sawback Lakes, cutthroat and Dolly Varden. These lakes are accessible by mountain trail about thirty miles from Banff. Fishing can also be obtained in numerous small streams within the Park and detailed information can be obtained from the park official and guides at Banff.

East of Calgary—Good catches of cutthroat and rainbow have been obtained on the Bow River at the mouth of Fish Creek and Highwood River. There is good pike fishing in Chestermere Lake twelve miles east of Calgary by good motor roads.

Brooks—There is good pike fishing in Lac Newell, seven miles south of Brooks.

Bassano—There is pike fishing in the Bow River south of the town.

Red Deer—At Sylvan Lake, sixteen miles by motor, west of the Red Deer, there is a summer resort at which there is good pike fishing. There is a beautiful sand beach here, cottages and boats can be rented. There is also good hotel accommodation. This lake can also be reached by the Canadian National Railway and Canadian Pacific Railway. At Pine Lake, twenty-five miles by good road, southeast of Red Deer, there is good pike and perch fishing. This lake is also accessible by motor road from Innisfail. Boats and hotel accommodation are available.

Lacombe—At Gull Lake, west of Lacombe, there is a summer resort and good pike fishing is available. Cottages and boats can be rented. This lake is accessible by motor and is eleven miles from Lacombe. Buffalo Lake, thirty miles east of Lacombe by motor and two miles from Mirror has good pike fishing. Boats are available at the Narrows, four miles from Mirror and at Rochon Sands eighteen miles by auto from Stettler. Cottages can be rented at the latter place.

Wetaskiwin and Millet—Pigeon Lake, twenty-five miles west of Millet and thirty miles from Wetaskiwin by auto, has pike and pickerel. There are good beaches at the south end of the lake, at Mulhurst and at Westerose. Summer cottages can be rented at Mulhurst and Westerose with a few boats.

West of Edmonton—Wabamun Lake has pike fishing. There are summer resorts at Seba, Wabamun and Kapasiwin at which cottages and boats may be rented. All are accessible by motor, fifty to sixty

[285]

miles from Edmonton, and also by Canadian National Railway. Lake Isle, near Wabamun, has pike, perch and pickerel fishing. Boats are obtainable at Ginford, four miles from Seba Beach.

Lac Ste. Anne, west of Edmonton—Has pike, pickerel and perch fishing. At Alberta Beach there is a summer resort at which hotel accommodation, cottages and boats may be obtained. This lake is accessible from Edmonton by motor forty-four miles, and also by Canadian National Railway.

Lac la Nonne and Lake Nakamun, north-west of Edmonton—Have pike, pickerel and perch. They are sixty and fifty-three miles respectively from Edmonton by motor road. Boats and cottages are obtainable.

Chip Lake, west of Edmonton—Has pike, pickerel and goldeyes, and is accessible by Canadian National Railway and by No. 16 Highway.

Edson, west of Edmonton—The tributaries of the Athabasca and McLeod Rivers have rainbow trout and grayling. Edson is accessible by motor over No. 16 Highway. Guides can be obtained at Edson, and Obed. These two streams form an excellent canoe route, commencing at the Canadian National Railway near the crossing of either river and journeying down stream to rail connection at White court, Smith or still further down at Athabasca.

Jasper Park—Fishing started in 1932 at Maligne Lake, in Jasper National Park, which hitherto was barren. Due to intensive stocking, this lake is now ready for excellent fishing and reports claim that the sport is unrivalled in this beauty spot.

North and East of Edmonton—In this locality are many good fishing lakes, the largest of which are Cold Lake, Frog Lake, Baptiste Lake, Lake St. Vincent, Floating Stone Lake, Fork Lake, Pinehurst Lake, Beaver Lake, Lac la Biche, Buck Lake, Skeleton Lake and Amisk Lake. Most of the lakes contain pike, pickerel and perch, while Cold Lake has excellent lake trout. Cold Lake has lake trout, pike and pickerel. At the lake are hotels, stores, cottages and boats. It is accessible by motor from St. Paul, Vermilion or Lloydminster. The largest trout taken by angling, 52½ pounds, and the largest pike 24, while the largst pickerel was 16 pounds. Trout have been taken on commercial fishing up to 70 pounds. At Cold Lake arrangements can be made to clean, ice and box all fish and hold in coolers at minimum charge. Lac la Biche has pike and pickerel. There is also hotel accommodation and some cottages and boats. This lake is accessible by Northern Alberta Railways and by motor via Colinton near Athabasca. Buck, Skeleton and Amisk Lakes have pike, pickerel and perch. They are accessible by Northern Alberta Railways and the two latter by motor via Colinton and Boyle. There is accommodation at Boyle. A few boats are available. Beaver Lake has pike, pickerel and perch. It is accessible from Lac la Biche by motor four miles. Lake St. Vincent has pike and perch and is ten miles from St. Paul by automobile. Boats are available. Accommodation can be secured at St. Paul. Moose Lake has pike, pickerel and perch. This lake is 30 miles from St. Paul. It has a lovely beach. Boats are available, also telephone, store, camping accommodation and hotel accommodation at Bonnyville. Muriel Lake has pike, pickerel and perch. Boats are scarce. This lake is accessible by motor 38 miles from St. Paul. Hotel accommodation is available at Bonnyville and St. Paul. Bonnyville is nine miles from the lake. Frog Lake has pike and perch. It is accessible by motor from Vermilion and Lloydminster. Boats are scarce. Baptiste Lake has pike, pickerel and perch. It is twelve miles by auto from Athabasca. There is an auto camp at the south end of the lake and hotel accommodation at Athabasca.

Northwest of Edmonton—Lesser Slave Lake has pike, pickerel and perch and Arctic grayling in the tributaries. Good angling is reported in Shaw Creek, Peace Creek and Martin River and Prairie Creek, near the Town of Slave Lake. Boats are available at all points on the south side of the lake. Accommodation at Slave Lake, Kinuso, Faust and Grouard. This lake is accessible by Northern Alberta Railways and No. 1 Highway.

BRITISH COLUMBIA

REGISTRATION OF FOREIGN CARS

Owners of automobiles brought into the Province for a period not exceeding six months, who are residents of the U.S.A., are not required to register their cars with the Provincial authorities, provided that they produce on demand, the Customs touring permit in respect to the automobile.

DRIVING REGULATIONS
BRIEFS FROM B.C. MOTOR VEHICLE ACT

Drivers of motor vehicles must be in possession of driving licence. Always carry it with you and show on demand of a police officer.

Speed Limit—Always drive in a careful and prudent manner. No person shall drive a vehicle on any highway so as to endanger the life or limb of any person or the safety of any property.

Driving in excess of twenty miles per hour in a city or municipality or thirty miles per hour in the country is considered evidence of driving in other than a prudent manner. The onus of proof that it is not driving to the common danger rests with the driver.

School Zones—Passing a school at more than fifteen miles per hour between 8 A. M. and 5 P. M. on school days is a serious offence.

Stop Signs—Full stop required wherever stop sign is displayed and before entering arterial highways. Also required to stop and remain standing ten feet behind street cars while passengers are boarding or alighting, except where safety islands are provided.

Parking on the main travelled portion of any highway is prohibited.

Right-of-Way—At intersections vehicles from the right have the right-of-way.

Mufflers must not be cut out or disconnected.

Spot-Lights—Only one spot-light allowed on vehicles. Beam must strike the ground within 100 feet and to right of centre of vehicle.

Signals—Standard arm and hand signals for turns and stops. Gongs, sirens and whistles prohibited, except by police, firemen and ambulances.

Stickers or any other non-transparent material prohibited upon upper half of front windshield, side wings, side or rear windows of car.

Windshields must be equipped with device for removing rain or other moisture.

Animals being transported must be protected in such a way that they will not fall or be thrown from the vehicle.

SUPPLEMENT

Centre Line—Crossing centre lines when overtaking another car, or on a curve or narrow road, is dangerous as well as illegal. Keep to the right.

Accidents—Report all accidents immediately to the nearest police station.

GOVERNMENT FERRIES

The Provincial Government owns or subsidizes a large number of automobile-ferries in connection with the Provincial highway system. The following ferries are operated on a fixed schedule:

Agassiz-Rosedale—Across Fraser River connecting Dewdney Trunk Road with Transcontinental Highway. Rate for ordinary car, 40c.

Castlegar—Across Columbia River on Nelson to Trail main road. Free except after scheduled hours.

Francois Lake—Connecting Burns Lake with points on south side of Francois Lake. Free except after scheduled hours.

Kelowna-Westbank—Crossing Okanagan Lake on Main Road, Vernon to Penticton, rate for ordinary car, 75c.

Ladner-Woodward—Crossing South Arm of Fraser River below New Westminster. Rate for ordinary car, 35c.

Nelson—West Arm of Kootenay Lake, connecting Kaslo with Nelson. Free.

Shuswap Lake—From Sicamous to various points on the lake and Seymour Arm. Rate, according to distance.

Sorrento-Scotch Creek—Across Shuswap Lake, making road connection from Notch Hill to Celista, etc. Free except after scheduled hours.

Arrowhead-Beaton—Upper Arrow Lake, 28 miles south-east of Revelstoke. Rate for ordinary car, $2.00.

Brentwood (Mill Bay)—Across Saanich Inlet, connecting Saanich Peninsula with the Island Highway (Malahat). Rate for ordinary car, $1.25.

Needles-Fauquier—Across the Columbia between Upper and Lower Arrow Lakes. Free except after scheduled hours.

CLOSING HOURS AT CUSTOMS

The hours kept at some of the principal ports of entry to British Columbia are as follows:

Pacific Highway—24-hour service.

Douglas (Year)—8:00 A. M. to 12:00 midnight.

Huntingdon-Sumas (Year)—8:00 A. M. to 12:00 midnight.

Boundary Bay (April 1st to June 30th)—7:00 A. M. to 12:00 midnight.

Boundary Bay (July 1st to September 15th)—6:00 A. M. to 12:00 midnight.

Boundary Bay (September 15th to October 15th)—7:00 A. M. to 12:00 midnight.

Boundary Bay (October 15th to March 31st)—8:00 A. M. to 12:00 midnight.

Osoyoos (November 1st to April 30th)—8:00 A.M. to 8:00 P. M.

Osoyoos (May 1st to October 31st)—7:00 A. M. to 11:00 P. M.

Kingsgate (Summer)—7:00 A. M. to 9:00 P. M.

Kingsgate (Winter)—8:00 A. M. to 6:00 P. M.

Paterson (April 1st to December 1st)—8:00 A. M. to 7:00 P. M.

Paterson (December 1st to April 1st)—8:00 A. M. to 5:00 P. M.

BRITISH COLUMBIA PARKS

PROVINCIAL PARKS

Mount Robson Park—Embraces 803 square miles in the heart of the Rocky Mountains. Mount Robson, highest peak in Canadian Rockies. Berg Lake, lodges and accommodation for visitors.

Strathcona Park—828 square miles, on Vancouver Island, reached by trail from Forbes Landing—magnificent scenery.

Garibaldi Park—460 square miles, reached by Pacific Great Eastern Railway from Squamish. Hotel accommodation at Daisy Lake.

Kokanee Park—100 square miles, reached by road and trail from Nelson and Kaslo.

Mount Assiniboine—20 square miles, in the Rocky Mountains, reached by trail from the Banff-Windermere Road.

SUPPLEMENT

DOMINION PARKS

Yoho Park—650 square miles, in the Rocky Mountains. Hotel and bungalow camp accommodations.

Kootenay Park—450 square miles, and extends on both sides of the Banff-Windermere Road. Bungalow and auto camps along road. Radium Hot Springs at southern boundary.

Glacier—468 square miles, in the Selkirk Mountains. Glacier House accommodation and Swiss guides for mountaineering parties.

Mount Revelstoke Park—95 square miles, reached by road from Revelstoke. Famous for ski-jump and winter sports.

CAMP-FIRE PERMITS

During the closed season (May 1 to October 1) a permit is necessary before any fire is kindled within a forest or woodland, even for the purpose of cooking or obtaining warmth.

Camp-fire permits are issued free of charge by the Provincial Police, Forestry Officer, Tourist Association, Automobile Club, and by many sporting goods stores.

All fires must be fully extinguished before leaving the vicinity.

Camp-fire permits must be endorsed by Municipal Clerks, or Fire Departments, if used within an organized municipality.

FISHING

KAMLOOPS

Within a short distance of the city of Kamloops there are sixty Alpine lakes in which the sporty Kamloops Trout may be caught.

LAKES

Showing the approximate mileages by road from Kamloops

Paul Lake, 12 miles north
Pinantan Lake, 19 miles north
Pemberton and Hyas Lakes, 3 miles north of Pinantan
Knouff Lake, 30 miles north
Dunn Lake, 56 miles north

Adams Lake, via North Thompson and Squam Bay, 56 miles
Adams Lake and River, via South Thompson and Squilax 49 miles
Niskonlith Lake, 8 miles north-west Shuswap
Little Shuswap Lake, 34 miles north-east
Big Shuswap Lake, Sorrento, 47 miles north-east
Fish Lake, 22 miles south

All these lakes are stocked under supervision of Government Fisheries Department.

FISHING—VANCOUVER ISLAND

Species:
　　Trout: Cutthroat, rainbow, steelhead.
　　Char: Dolly Varden.
　　Black bass.
　　Salmon: Spring (Tyee), cohoe, grilse.
Open Season:
　　Trout:
　　　　March 1—November 14.
　　　　Steelhead all year.
　　Bass:
　　　　July 1—March 31.
　　Salmon:
　　　　All year.
Limit of Catch:
　　Trout species: 15 a day.
　　Black bass: 15 a day.
　　Salmon species: 5 a day.
Size of Fish:
　　No fish under 8 inches to be taken.
　　　　No fish in Cowichan River under 10 inches to be taken. (Keep
　　　　hands wet when handling these small fish.)
Methods of Fishing:
　　For trout and bass:
　　　　Fly from boat, wading or from bank, also trolling from boat.
　　Steelhead trout:
　　　　Spinning, or fly, by wading rivers.

SUPPLEMENT

Flies:

    Trout: Standard makes and local, to suit season.

    Grilse: Bucktail flies and Polar Bear.

    Salmon: Bucktail.

Best Season:

Salmon:

    Cohoe: fly fishing: August, September and October.

Trout:

    April, May; September and October.

    No fish roe of any kind nor roe compounds to be used while fishing for or catching trout.

Campbell River:

    The fishing at Campbell River is excellent in May, June and July for "Springs." Fly fishing for Cohoe from July to the end of October. August to the 15th of September is the Tyee season.

Salmon:

Cohoe:

    July to October 30.

Tyee:

    August to September 15.

MILEAGE TABLES

NORTH SHORE VANCOUVER HARBOR

	Miles from Auto Club via Bridge
Capilano Canyon	9
Capilano Intake	16
Caulfeilds	18
Cypress Park	17
Deep Cove	11
Dollarton	10
Eagle Harbour	19.3
Fishermen's Cove	20.1

Miles from
Auto Club
via Bridge

Glen Eagles Golf Course	21.2
Grouse Mountain Chalet	18.5
Horseshoe Bay	22.5
Kew Beach	19
Lynn Valley	8.5
West Vancouver	12.6
West Bay	16
Whytecliff	24

MAINLAND FROM VANCOUVER

Miles from
Vancouver

Abbotsford	44.5
Agassiz (ferry to Rosedale)	74.5
Aldergrove	35.5
Alexandra Bridge	131
Armstrong (via Salmon Arm)	376
Ashcroft	227
Banff—	
Via Revelstoke	531
Via Banff-Windermere, Nelson, Kamloops	968
Via Princeton	860
Barkerville	513
Boston Bar	147
Boundary Bay—	
Via Woodward's Landing	23
Via New Westminster	42
Bralorne	269
Bridge River	237
Burns Lake	688
Calgary (via Nelson)	1054
Calgary (via Revelstoke)	617

SUPPLEMENT

SUPPLEMENT

Miles from
Vancouver

Radium Hot Springs 888
Revelstoke 434
   (C.P.R. ship cars between Revelstoke and Golden at
   special rates.)
Rock Creek 497
Rosedale (ferry to Agassiz) 73.5
Rossland 607
Rykerts, via Okanagan and Nelson 701
Salmon Arm 353
Sicamous 390
Slocan—
   Via Trail 678
   Via Edgewood 510
Smithers 783
Soda Creek 398
Sorrento 331
Spence's Bridge 201
Spuzzum Toll Gate 131
St. Elmo 93
Trail, via Kamloops 606
Vanderhoof 602
Vernon 358
Victoria, V.I., via ferry 72
Westbank, ferry to Kelowna 395
West Summerland 417
White Rock—
   Via Johnston Road 30
   Via Campbell River Road 35
Williams Lake 379
Windermere 869
Yale 117

SUPPLEMENT

Miles from
Vancouver

Vancouver	0
Blaine	32
Bellingham	56
Mt. Vernon	83
Everett	120
Seattle	148
Tacoma	180
Olympia	211.5
Chehalis	246.5
Longview	292.5
Portland	344.5
Salem	395
Eugene	464.5
Roseburg	538.5
Grants Pass	616.5
Medford	648.5
Ashland	660.5
Yreka	705.5
Weed	733.5
Mt. Shasta	743
Dunsmuir	751.5
Lamoine	774
Redding	812.5
Red Bluff	844
Chico	885.5
Marysville	933
Sacramento	985.5
Stockton	1033
Modesto	1062
Merced	1100
Fresno	1155.5
Tulare	1201

Miles from
Vancouver

Bakersfield	1254
Gorman	1309.5
San Fernando	1354.5
Los Angeles	1377.5
Pomona	1413
Riverside	1436.5
Elsinore	1465.5
Escondido	1522.5
San Diego	1557.5
Tia Juana	1575

VANCOUVER ISLAND

Miles from
Victoria

Alberni	132
Brentwood	14
Campbell River	175
Cameron Lake	113
Chemainus	54
Comox	150
Courtenay	146
Cowichan Bay	35
Cowichan Lake	60
Cumberland	145
Deep Cove	22
Duncan	41
Elk Lake	8
Forbes Landing	190
Great Central Lake	143
Jordan River	42
Ladysmith	61
Langford	8
Maple Bay	44

SUPPLEMENT

MEMORANDA

MEMORANDA

MEMORANDA

MEMORANDA

MEMORANDA

MEMORANDA

MEMORANDA